BRIGHT

BEOWULF

Intelligent Education

INFLUENCE PUBLISHERS

Nashville, Tennessee

BRIGHT NOTES: Beowulf

www.BrightNotes.com

ISBN: 978-1-645420-36-1 (Paperback)

ISBN: 978-1-645420-37-8 (eBook)

Published in accordance with the U.S. Copyright Office Orphan Works and Mass Digitization report of the register of copyrights, June 2015.

Originally published by Monarch Press.

George Quasha, 1965

2019 Edition published by Influence Publishers.

Interior design by Lapiz Digital Services. Cover Design by Thinkpen Designs.

Printed in the United States of America.

Library of Congress Cataloging-in-Publication Data forthcoming.

Names: Intelligent Education

Title: BRIGHT NOTES: Beowulf

Subject: STU004000 STUDY AIDS / Book Notes

CONTENTS

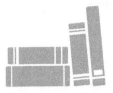

INTRODUCTION

....

THE ROMANS

Writing in the first quarter of the eighth century, the Anglo-Saxon historian Bede informs us that the first Roman to reach Britain was Julius Caesar. From other sources we know that Caesar invaded Britain twice: in 55 B.C. and 54 B.C. The first invasion was little more than a reconnaissance, lasting only about three weeks; the second was an ambitious undertaking employing large forces. In both enterprises the Romans experienced a heavy loss of ships owing to ignorance of the Channel tides, and were discomfited by the mobility of British chariot warfare. On the second invasion - a failure in terms of the forces employed - some alliances were made and hostages taken; but no Roman troops were left behind. Subsequently, Caesar's energies were diverted to Gallic revolt and then to civil war, and thoughts of the possible occupation of Britain were abandoned. Almost a century would elapse before the conquest of Britain under Claudius.

THE CELTS

The inhabitants of Britain were of Celtic extraction, Celtic peoples having migrated into Europe as early as the ninth century B.C. The Britons were related to the Gauls and as such were certainly no strangers to either the Romans or Julius Caesar. Indeed, military operations had been conducted against the Celts by the Romans from the earliest times and the Celtic peoples inhabiting Northern Italy had provided an important source of manpower for the armies of Hannibal during his invasion of the Roman peninsula in 218-203 B.C. As we shall see, the unsubdued Celtic peoples, e.g., the Picts who inhabited present-day Scotland, and the Scots, who inhabited - until the third century A.D. - present-day Ireland, eventually overran a large part of Roman Britain.

The Roman conquest and occupation of Britain, begun in A.D. 43 by the emperor Claudius, was consolidated in the reign of the emperor Hadrian by the building of Hadrian's Wall in A.D. 121 as a bulwark against the unruly tribes (the Picts and Scots) of Northern Britain. Generally, the failure of Caesar's invasions is indicative of weaknesses in the Roman Empire that would not become obvious or apparent for several centuries. Caesar's failure on the North parallels Roman operations in the East, where the millionaire Crassus was killed in a war with the Parthians - an exhaustive war in an area which would, like Britain, eventually prove to be more troublesome than Imperial Rome cared to admit. The progress of history is uneven and for both the Britons under Roman rule and the Romans themselves there were to be happier times. From the establishment of Hadrian's Wall in the second century until well into the fourth century, the Britons were to enjoy peace and prosperity. The northern invaders had been largely constrained and it was not until the third century that the Romans were required to build coastal defense against the sea-raiders, the Saxons. Roman writers of this period employ the term Saxon as a generic classification of several sea-faring peoples, including the Angles, Saxons and Jutes. The first mention of the Angles (from which we get the word England) occurs in Germania, written in the first century A.D. by the Roman historian Tacitus. Tacitus' reference to the "Anglii" is rather nebulous: he refers to them merely as an "island people."

DECLINE AND INVASION

The time of troubles of Roman Britain may be said to have begun in the middle of the fourth century when the Roman garrisons were withdrawn for operations against continental barbarians who were beginning to make inroads upon the Empire. Clearly, the Romans did not regard Britain as an integral part of their empire and were willing to sacrifice it, just as lands east of the Rhine were given up centuries earlier when they became too difficult and costly to defend. The fate of the Britons seems to parallel the fate of the Romans to a degree, because both peoples lost that spirit which characterized the Germanic peoples of this period - the Roman symptom was easily noticed by Tacitus three centuries before. Subtly contrasting the Roman life of "bread and circuses" with the German, Tacitus describes the virtuous and vigorous life enjoyed by the German tribes; he extols their conception of the family as the basic unit of society. By demonstrating the advantages of the more stoic or "natural" man, Tacitus was pointing out the dangers which existed for a society devoted to pleasure. Tacitus' moral might just as easily have been drawn for the Britons themselves because they had become stultified under peaceful centuries of Roman rule and protection. When the Britons appealed to Rome for aid against their enemies, the emperor Honorius replied that he could not send aid and that they must look after themselves. According to Bede, it was Honorius' observation that the Britons suffered attack because they lacked the spirit to defend themselves.

Hadrian's Wall, the bulwark against the savage tribes of the North, was overwhelmed by a united force of Picts and Scots in 367 and almost all of Britain was overrun. Roman superiority was reestablished briefly by Theodosius two years later, but the internal affairs in the Roman empire - notably power struggles between military commanders - left Britain undefended for long periods of time. As an example, a Roman military commander in Gaul, Magnus Maximus, determined to seize the Western Empire from the Emperor Gratian and removed almost all Roman troops from Britain in 383. This operation left Hadrian's Wall completely undefended and ended its usefulness as a container of the Picts and Scots. Thereafter, Roman control of the island wavered until the Britons were left to the mercy of the invaders entirely.

THE ANGLO-SAXON PERIOD

Traditions of the invasions of Britain may be grouped into two categories, the Welsh and the English. The best source for the Welsh tradition is *De Excidu et Conquestu Britanniae* (*On the Invasion and Conquest of Britain*), composed in the middle of the sixth century by a teacher and religious figure, Gildas. Although there are many errors in the work, and its function is chiefly religious rather than historical, it suggests certain facts about which we would otherwise know nothing. *De Excidu* is apparently Bede's source for the account of the earliest Anglo-Saxon invasions of Britain. In *The History of the English Church and Peoples*, Bede relates that Anglo-Saxon contingents were invited by Vortigern - a fifth-century king of the Britons - to help in the defense against the Picts and Scots. After the successful conclusion of a war against them, however, Vortigern found that his allies did not wish to leave, nor could he dislodge them. Eventually, the Britons were able to defeat the mercenaries and, according to Gildas, this was followed by a brief period of peace.

This Vortigern is the king to whom Gildas refers as superbus Tyrannus. On the whole Bede's work integrates the work of Gildas, other legends, accounts and chronicles with time and place, making a rather more definite - though possibly not a more accurate work.

TRADITIONS

English traditions are found in the Old English poem *The Fight at Finnsburg* and also in the so-called Finn **Episode**, contained in *Beowulf*. The general tradition is that King Hnaef of Denmark and his warriors visited Finn, king of Frisia. A band of Finn's men attacked Hnaef and his men in their mead-hall and a fight ensued which lasted five days. During this period no Dane fell and their attackers were about to retire. Here, unfortunately, the poem breaks off. From *Beowulf*, we learn that Hnaef is eventually killed and peace is temporarily concluded between the two groups, the Danes receiving their own hall and lands. The Danes - except Hengest, their new leader - went home for the winter, later returning with reinforcements. In a subsequent battle, Finn is killed.

THE ANGLO-SAXON CHRONICLE

The Anglo-Saxon Chronicle, written in Old English and Latin, is an important source for the partial verification of Welsh and

English traditions, but, as the reader may already suspect, there is to be no such thing in the study of Anglo-Saxon history as absoluteness. In most of Western Europe yearly diaries, or chronicles, were kept in which the significant happenings of the year were recorded. Obviously such records would be very uneven, some years being passed by completely or noted by only a sentence, other years treated extensively according to the taste, disposition or interests of the chronicler. *The Anglo-Saxon Chronicle* is actually a compilation of separate chronicles, seven in number, of which six are written in Old English and one written in a combination of Old English and Latin. There is evidence to suggest that chronicles were being kept in England as early as the eighth century, although the earliest manuscript of *the Anglo-Saxon Chronicle* dates from c. 891.

In one of the texts of the *Chronicle*, an account is given under the dates 449–473 of a kingdom established in Kent by Hengest, his brother Horsa, and his son Aesic. This also includes an account of battles against the Welsh and the arrival of other chieftains: "456. In this year Hengest and Aesic fought the Britons at a place called Crayford and slew four companies there. The Britons then gave up Kent and fled in fear to London."

We notice that the *Chronicle* begins with a date. The manuscript was probably first marked off in lines for each year which was to be filled in by the chronicler. Obviously, the entry would depend upon the amount of information available to the compiler; thus many spaces were left blank. After the date would follow the Old English word Her, meaning, literally, "at this place in the annals." The process of gradual recording is probably the main reason for the use of an adverb of place rather than time in a book of annals. The *Chronicle* has value as history and also occasionally as literature. For example, the entry of 755 (written at least as late as 784 and probably inserted in the earlier year's space) gives an account of Cynewulf and Cyneheard (of the latter's murder of the former), and the little story is often called the first short story because of its delicate denouement.

OTHER RECORDS

The English and Welsh traditions, although suggestive of historical facts, have to the present time provided little for the historian except sources for speculation and inquiry. Continental sources are largely fragmentary and do little more than to suggest the most general outline of the history of the Early Anglo-Saxon period. The historian Zosimus records that in the fifth century, the Britons seceded from the Roman Empire, took up arms and defeated the barbarians. Zosimus' reference for this account is believed to be a work (which was subsequently lost) written by the Greek historian Olympidorus, who was contemporary with the events. Other references - and they are few in number - are equally indefinite.

ANGLO-SAXON KINGDOMS - COMITATUS

That the Anglo-Saxon invasions were largely successful, however, is not open to dispute, because by the beginning of the seventh century there were almost a dozen separate Anglo-Saxon kingdoms in Southern England alone. As we have noted, the historical events of this period seem to be veiled in nebulosity and this is perhaps due to the small-scale conditions of the invasions. Of great help in understanding the character of the Anglo-Saxon institutions of the period is the account given by Tacitus in his Germania. Although written several centuries before the German tribes were to invade Britain, it seems likely (from other evidences) that Germanic society had not changed too significantly to preclude the validity of his observations. We are informed that the Germans, considered the family the basic unit of their society, were industrious, warlike, and chose their kings for birth and their generals for merit. Although slavery existed and it was possible for a German to sell or gamble himself into slavery, the social structure was not rigid and poorer Germans could rise by demonstrating their bravery and valor in battle. An institution noticed by Tacitus is the comitatus (in his term) by which a youth would attach himself to a strong leader: "... such lads attach themselves to men of mature strength and strong valor." (Germania.) This institution is almost the precursor on a lessor scale of certain feudal institutions and does form the basis for the lord-thane relationships which we will subsequently observe in *Beowulf*. The obligation of the lord was to provide his retainers with goods and bounty in exchange for their services. It was considered dishonorable for a lord to be outdone in bravery by one of his thanes and it was equally dishonorable for a thane to leave the battlefield upon which his lord remained. In the *Nibelungenlied* we see evidences of this in "comrades of the sword," and in Anglo-Saxon England this tradition would persist until well into the tenth century.

We may see that the numerous chieftains or lords with personal bands of followers would, in a sense, represent no more than "adventurers," and as such would not be at great pains to provide history with a record of their accomplishments or deeds.

CHRISTIANITY

According to Bede, the British king Lucius sent a letter to Eleutherius and asked to become a Christian (A.D. 156). The *Chronicle* gives the date as 167, but in any case it is obvious that many Celts had become Christianized during the Roman occupations. The conversion of the Anglo-Saxons began in 597 when Pope Gregory the Great sent St. Augustine (not to be confused with another St. Augustine, author of the City of God) to England with instructions to proceed slowly in his conversion of the Anglo-Saxons. The institutions of the English were to be slowly and patiently transformed, a distinct contrast to the manner which would subsequently be employed by the "Knight of the Christian Faith," Charlemagne, when he gave his subjects the choice of Christianity or the sword. This deliberate policy suggested by Pope Gregory goes far in explaining the late persistence of Germanic traditions in Britain and, as we shall see later, accounts for many a curious admixture of pagan and Christian elements in *Beowulf* and other Old English literature.

After Augustine had converted Kent, Canterbury became the center of the Roman Church activity in Britain early in the seventh century. The Synod of Whitby in 661 marked the first step in the gradual ascendancy of the Roman Church in England and although there was some backsliding toward heathenism or heterodoxy, the influence of the church gradually extended itself. Canterbury, York and other monasteries became centers of learning and of Latin and Greek scholarship. As we might remember from later English history, the geography of Britain - its insularity - tended to permit the English a lifeless subject to papal control than that of their continental neighbors.

ARCHAEOLOGICAL EVIDENCE

While coins and inscriptions and dwelling sites constitute most of the body of remnants of Romano-British civilization, there is little similar evidence of Anglo-Saxon civilization. Since the Anglo-Saxons built their houses of wood, left few inscriptions and did not manufacture their own coins, there is little left to the archaeologist but objects left in the graves of the dead. Generally, the Anglo-Saxons buried their dead in shallow graves and did not mark them by any special mound or means. However, the pattern of the already uncovered graves indicates (because of their sparseness in the North) that the Anglo-Saxon conquest of Northern England was little more than an imposition of rule upon a basic Celtic population, unlike Southern England which became inhabited by the Anglo-Saxons extensively.

PLACE-NAMES

Like archaeological evidence left by the Anglo-Saxons, the evidence of place-names is not such that it may easily be assigned a chronology. However, when a place-name is mentioned by Bede we know that it is at least as old as the eighth century, and scholars may reasonably infer that it is much older. Generally, place-names in Britain have remained the same (although there are significant exceptions) except in the cases where a new language and consequently new names have been introduced through invasion. One of the most important of the types of place-names are names that end in ingas. This suffix means "follower of," and is usually combined with a personal name. As an example, Hastings, derived from the Old English, is interpreted as "the followers of Haesta." This name was originally applied to a group of people who might be spread over a very large area, pointing to a time in English history when the groups of settlers were more important than where they lived. Significantly, place-names are more numerous in areas which lie off the main routes of communication. As we might suspect, these areas would be less subject to the ups and downs of invasions, and less influenced by external conditions. Thus, a certain conservativism would be evidenced by place-names.

ANGLO-SAXON CULTURE

The Anglo-Saxons, like their Germanic forebears mentioned in Tacitus' Germania, probably lived in a tribal state for some time after they arrived in Britain. Originally, the tribe-structure of Anglo-Saxon society was the development of an extremely integrated clan-structure. The tribe had only two classes: the aristocracy (or earls) who claimed descent from a founder of the tribe; and the plebeians and proletarians (or churls) who claimed no such descent and included bondsmen and captives. In addition there were a few men of exception, called freemen, whose status was uncertain and who held this distinction, apparently, as some sort of reward or special favor.

The head of the tribe was the hereditary king; his genealogy was commonly traced from Woden, king of the gods. To advise the king there was a council of elders, the witan. This institution persisted late in Britain under the name witenagemot and a few modern historians have traced the British parliament back to it. It will be noted that the witan or witenagemot gained considerable political strength for itself which did not place it outside the general tendency from the sixth century onward; that is, the condensation of power of the witan steadily grew during the half-millenium before the year 1000; the power of the aristocracy waxed and waned in long cycles; and the power of the Anglo-Saxon kings was chiefly dependent upon the residual principle - that is, if the king did not possess the ability to take advantage of the power condensation, it went elsewhere.

The importance of the individual in Anglo-Saxon society was a direct function of his social class. As we shall see in *Beowulf*, the vendetta or revenge motive was perfectly acceptable as a means of "law," and generally this holds true for most primitive tribes. In the transition from the law of vendetta to the rule of law, however, the wergild or blood-money is an interesting example. The law of the wergild specified that a person who had suffered damages through the killing of a relative might exact a sum of money from the murderer as an expiation of the crime. The value of an earl was assessed higher than a freeman and a freeman was assessed higher than a churl. And, of course, men were assessed higher than women of a corresponding class.

From the assessment of women for wergild, the conclusion may rightly be drawn that women were valued less than men by the Anglo-Saxons. From *Beowulf*, it is easily inferred that women are of only slight importance: there is only one female character who assumes any sort of life at all, Wealhtheow, Hrothgar's wife. The Anglo-Saxon woman was expected to be domestic and moral. To the Anglo-Saxon mind, apparently, this was the limitation of her ability. She was, however, accorded her full legal rights and a certain respect that approached idealization. From *Beowulf* we learn that it was the function of some aristocratic women to act as peacemakers or arbitrators, a role which - to the Anglo-Saxons - they seemed singularly well fitted.

From the literature of the period - and as we shall see in *Beowulf* - there are very few glimpses of the daily life of the so-called average person. The coast-guardsman represents the most ordinary character we shall meet in *Beowulf* and little is made of him, his life, or preferences. Only his function is important. Like the television dramas of today, Old English literature presents on a superficial level too little of the Anglo-Saxon's occupations and hopes, and too much, perhaps, of hating and violence. Between the deserts of man's grim struggle, however, stand a few oases of morality and aspiration. *Beowulf* provides a better view of man's hopes and preoccupations with the meaning of life (a preoccupation which basically must be positive, since negative preoccupation would merely demonstrate its own futility) than do, for example, The Fight at Finnsburg, or The Battle of Brunanburh, which present little more in this sense than a series of grim specters.

SUTTON HOO

In 1939 at a private estate in southeastern Suffolk, the remains of a ship-burial that occurred sometime in the middle of the seventh century were uncovered. The name of the estate is Sutton Hoo burial-ship. This, of course, was not the first burial ship to be discovered by archaeologists. The discovery did constitute a remarkable find, however, because of the richness in cultural and material objects found in the site.

The burial-ship had never been to see perhaps but reflected an old Scandinavian custom of setting the dead hero or king afloat, surrounded with treasure. This was based upon the notion that the dead were undertaking a journey during which (or at the end of which) they would require the treasure and belongings accompanying them. The "journeying of the dead" is a notion common to many mythologies, and we remember the Egyptian bark of the dead as well as Charon's Ferry across the Styx in Greek mythology.

It seems likely that the Sutton Hoo burial-ship served as a cenotaph or memorial to some Anglo-Saxon king who was buried elsewhere. Scholars consider that the king may be identified as the East Anglian King Anna (died 654) or Aethelhere (died 655). This would date the burial ship at a point in time less than one century earlier than the composition of *Beowulf*. For this reason, then, does the Sutton Hoo discovery recommend itself to our attention.

From a consideration of the effects found in the burial ship it is obvious that the Anglo-Saxons had developed a sophisticated culture. The workmanship of the gold objects found is of a very high degree, and other objects, such as a small harp, signify that music and poetry held a favored position in the court life of the times. In addition there are many items of solid gold and silver, gold and silver coins (which were useful in determining the date of the burial), and other objects which imply a high level of material wealth. The presence of Christian objects (and the absence of a body) imply that the pagan customs were rapidly being superseded by Christian beliefs.

Before the discovery of Sutton Hoo, the account of the funeral of Scyld Sceafing in *Beowulf* was considered merely a romantic flight of the poet's imagination. The interpretation given to Anglo-Saxon society tended to emphasize the primitiveness and coarseness of it (regarding the Anglo-Saxons as having progressed no further than Tacitus' Germans), but today we see that this interpretation was erroneous. The interested reader is referred to the July 16, 1951 issue of Life (XXXII, pp. 82–85) for some interesting and informative full-color pictures of the burial ship which are representative of the variegated and sophisticated Anglo-Saxon seventh-century society.

The significance of Sutton Hoo in our study of Old English literature is very great and has not been exhausted by scholars. Prof. Bessinger has explored the significance of the harp in relation to poetry (see Bibliography for his article and his impressive recording of Caedmon's Hymn with the harp). Prof. Wrenn has examined the aspects of the Sutton Hoo evidence as regards *Beowulf* (see Bibliography).

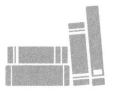

BEOWULF

THE ENGLISH LANGUAGE

INTRODUCTION

It is acceptable to refer to the literature which we will be examining subsequently as either Old English or Anglo-Saxon. Academically, "Old English" is preferred since it implies a continuity of the language and literature of England from the earliest to the present times. As we have seen, the word "England" is derived from "Angle-land," although Anglo-Saxon writers who wrote in Latin referred to their language as Lingua Anglica or Lingua Saxonica. Alfred the Great, writing in the ninth century, referred to his language as Englisc.

BEOWULF

Old English, which refers to the language of both the Angles and the Saxons (since it was the same), persisted as a written means of expression for some time after the spoken word had made its transition from Old to Middle English late in the eleventh and in the beginning of the twelfth centuries. Historically, English is a derivative of the ancestral Indo-European language (also called Indo-Germanic), which was probably spoken before recorded history around Lithuania and southern Russia. The language divided into nine groups (probably as early as 2500 B.C.): Indian, Iranian, Armenian, Hellenic, Albanian, Italic, Balto-Slavic, Germanic (Teutonic), and Celtic. Each of these groups or branches subdivided into the languages which we know as the moderns. The Teutonic branch divided into East Teutonic, North Teutonic, and West Teutonic. (For a full account of the general development of and origin of Indo-European languages, see Bibliography under Linguistic Background).

DIVISIONS OF OLD ENGLISH

Generally Old English is divided into two periods: (1) Early Old English - from A.D. 700 to 900; (2) Late Old English - from A.D. 900 to about 1100. In our study of Old English language and literature, we are concerned almost exclusively with Late Old English, for the only reliable document we have from the Early Old English is King Alfred's translation of Cura Pastoralis. Even this document, from late in the Early English period, shows that the language is transitional to Late Old English Classical Old English, therefore, is the Late Old English of Aelfric in prose and *Beowulf* in poetry. Often texts were written earlier, but the form in which they presently exist is that of a scribe's version of the Late Old English period, usually from around the year A.D. 1000. (The student should keep in mind that dates assigned to manuscripts are constantly being debated by scholars, for linguistic, literary, cultural and archeological evidence must be weighed and compared before even an approximate date of composition can be agreed upon).

CLASSICAL OLD ENGLISH

The center of Late Old English, or the classical language in which *Beowulf* is written, is that of King Alfred the Great in the southern and southwestern region of Wessex (West Saxon). Modern English is not actually derived specifically from this language but from the East Midland (Anglian) dialect of King Offa the Mercian. (It is easy to see that the term Old English, while justly indicating the continuity of the literature, is something of a misnomer in terms of linguistics.) At this time there were four major dialects: (1) West Saxon: the Saxon dialect of the Wessex kingdom (the other dialects produced no writing that remains); (2) Kentish: Southeastern England; (3) Mercian: West Midland, from which Modern English derives; (4) Northumbrian. (See map.) Most grammars take the language of Aelfric as the authority.

It is interesting to note that the Celtic language continued to be spoken throughout the Anglo-Saxon period in the more remote parts of Britain. Another language, Old Norse, appeared in the latter half of the ninth century, brought over by Viking raiders. This language also persisted for a few centuries but neither language - Celtic or Old Norse - was so sufficiently general as to make its effects felt in the literature.

THE ALPHABET

In *Beowulf* it will be seen that Hrothgar is able to read runes that are inscribed on the hilt of a sword presented him as a trophy. The runic alphabet was introduced into Britain by the Anglo-Saxons themselves and enjoyed a somewhat limited popularity. The Latin alphabet, which was capable of rendering most Old English sounds, was used, generally, and with only slight modification. Runic inscriptions, however, have been found and dated as early as the fourth century A.D. in Denmark and it has been found that the same series of runes came into use in Western Germany perhaps a century and a half later. Scholars have suggested that the runic alphabet was derived from a North Italic alphabet by the Eruli, a people who inhabited Denmark from the middle of the fifth century A.D. Without going too deeply into the development of the runes, the "English" Runic Alphabet progressed geographically from Scandinavia along the coast of the North Sea and was then brought to England by the Anglo-Saxons.

These runes are called Anglo-Frisian and are found on two score or so inscriptions on coins, burial objects, etc. In addition there are a few stones bearing runes in the north of England. The last English runic inscriptions belong to the tenth century and they seem not to have been used much for monuments after the Danish invasion in 865. With the decline of the runic alphabet, of course, coincided the rise of the Latin alphabet.

The student of Old English need only familiarize himself with a few fundamentals before beginning to decipher the original texts. (For those interested, it is possible to begin reading almost immediately with the aid of a translation. Below we will have occasion to compare a few lines of Old and Modern English.) For example, the thorn sign p stood for a vowel sound equal to that in our that or than. The different th sounds of then and thin, while originally differentiated, came to be represented interchangeably by the thorns p and d. (Wherever the student reads th in the following Old English poetry, a thorn appeared originally!) The Old English y was pronounced like German u - a sound which has passed out of modern English.

THE LORD'S PRAYER: TWO VERSIONS

To see some of the differences and similarities it will be helpful to glance at the two texts of the *Lord's Prayer*, one of the Old English versions and the familiar one found in the King James version of the Bible, Matthew 6:9-13.

Faeder ure thu the eart on heofonum si thin nama gehalgod. Tobecume thin rice. Gewurthe thin willa on eorthan swa swa on heofonum. Urne gedaeghwamlican hlaf syle us to daeg. And forgyf us ure gyltas swa swa we forgyfath urum gyltendum. And ne gelaed thu us on costnunge ac alys us of yfele. Sothlice.

Our father which art in heaven, hallowed be thy name. Thy kingdom come. Thy will be done in earth, as it is in heaven. Give us this day our daily bread. And forgive us our debts, as we forgive our debtors. And lead us not into temptation, but deliver us from evil ... Amen.

We can immediately see that Modern English has become quite a different language, and this development, as we shall see, is the result of a complex process of linguistic influences. In the above we can also see that the changes are largely orthographic (in spelling). Hlaf has become loaf - the h is dropped and the vowel changed. Faeder is father. On the other hand, some words have been replaced: costnung (seen here in the dative case, costnunge) is now the French importation temptation.

Grammatically Old English differed quite a bit from Modern English. It was, like Latin, Greek and Modern German as well as Russian, a more highly inflected language; that is, among other things, its nouns took case endings, its verbs took more person and number endings, its adjectives took endings, etc. There were four cases of nouns: nominative, genitive, dative, and accusative. Adjectives took the same ending plus the instrumental case. (We remember that modern English has only two cases for nouns, including the possessive, and none for adjectives.) For example, heofonum (heaven), used above, is the dative singular (object of the preposition on, meaning in). Forgyfath (forgive) is the first person plural of the verb.

Grammatical relationships were expressed by the special endings. In Modern English, grammatical relationships are expressed by a much more rigid **syntax** or word order than Old English required. Thus, in Old English poetry, word order could be altered severely to meet metrical requirements. An example of the differences can be seen in the following: urne gedaeghwamlican hlaf syle us is reversed in Modern English Give us our daily bread.

VOCABULARY DIFFERENCES

Old English, like all languages, borrowed words from foreign languages: it borrowed from Latin and Norse, for example. But basically it was unilingual in that it formed new words by compounds made up of its own roots. Note the following process: mod - heart or spirit or mind (which became Modern English mood); modig - spirited, by addition of - ig (roughly equivalent to - y in adjective endings: blodig means bloody); modcraeft - intelligence, by addition of craeft, meaning "skill" or "craft"; thus it means literally "skill of mind"; unmod - depression, by addition of the prefix un; guthmodig - of warlike mind or warlike, by addition of guth, meaning war.

The fact that the majority of Old English words were of native origin is perhaps the greatest difference between that language and Modern English. Only about fourteen percent of the words in Webster's *New World Dictionary* have been derived from Old English. Of course many of the frequently used words are those from Anglo-Saxon, words like I, the, man, woman, and, loaf, etc. Thus the most frequently used thousand words in our speaking vocabularies are derived from Old English to the extent of over sixty percent.

THE DEVELOPMENT OF MODERN ENGLISH

The periods of the development of the English language are generally stated as: Old English or Anglo-Saxon - 449 to 1066; Middle English - 1066 to 1485; Modern English - 1485 to present day. These are, of course, only convenient dates, for the development of a language is slow and complex. The significant dates to keep in mind as regards this development are:

43 to 499: The Romans occupied the island of Britain. They civilized and Christianized many of the Celts who lived there. After the withdrawal of the Romans (for the Empire, under attacks of the Barbarians, needed its armies), tribes from the northern coast of Europe invaded. They spoke dialects of Low West Germanic, were pagans, and were much less civilized than the Romans. We group them thus: the Angles (to the east and north of the island); the Saxons (to the south and west); and the Jutes (in the southeast).

499: This is the date usually assigned to the original Anglo-Saxon invasions. The Roman occupation left relatively little impact on the language of the island. The invading tribes defeated the Celts, fought among themselves, formed independent kingdoms, began to form diplomatic relationships, and were converted to Christianity. Records show that they began to write their language sometime in the seventh century. The influence of Christianity was vital to the course of development the peoples of the island were to take. In 664 the Synod of Whitby resolved many of the differences between the religious positions of the North and the South, of the Irish leadership and that of Rome. Due largely to the influence of Christianity, the language was written by the clerics in monasteries. After the death of Alfred the Great (849–899), the island was overrun by Danes and Norwegians. In 1017 Canute (Cnut), who was to become King of Denmark, held the English throne. But the sturdy English culture prevailed. The last Anglo-Saxon king was Edward the Confessor (1041–1066)

1066: This is the date of the Norman Conquest, led by Duke William. For several hundred years after this, the kings of

England spoke French as their first language. French became the aristocratic language and it profoundly influenced the course of Middle and Modern English. A great change took place in the language after this, as we shall see below. Over ten thousand French words were introduced into the language, particularly in the areas most in the hands of the aristocracy: law, government, military, art, medicine, etc. Some French words, as we saw above with temptation in place of costnung, took the place of the Old English. Often Old English, French, and Latin words took on subtleties of difference, as in holy, sacred, and consecrated. But by the time of Chaucer (1340–1400), English had become the language of literature and society. As in Old English, there were several major dialects: East Midland became preeminent for several reasons: it was spoken in London; it was used by William Caxton, the first English printer, when he set up his press in 1476; and it was Chaucer's language. But some major literature was written in other dialects: for example, Piers Plowman, Sir Gawain and the Green Knight, and Pearl.

1485: This is the date of the accession of the first of the Tudors to the English throne, Henry VII, and is a convenient date for the beginning of Modern English. Of course Modern English is not one language and has itself gone through a complex process of development. It is sometimes divided: Early Modern English - 1485 to 1700; Late Modern English - after 1700.

Early Modern English, the language of the sixteenth and seventeenth centuries, is not by any means the language we speak but it is very familiar to us, for it is the language of the King James Version of the Bible (quoted above) and of Shakespeare. Pronunciation and usage have changed a great deal since then, and it is unlikely that Sir Laurence Olivier or Sir John Gielgud could even be understood by Shakespeare's audience. Late Modern English came with the eighteenth century and attempts to formalize the language. In 1603 the first English dictionary had been published, but the age of dictionaries followed the publication in 1755 of Samuel Johnson's English Dictionary. The spirit of the sixteenth and seventeenth century had been one of adventure and seeking to discover new realms: hence Shakespeare's "explosion" of the language into new words and ways of writing. In the neo-classical eighteenth century the direction was toward the formal. Academicians sought to find a grammar for a language which was thought to be undignified without it. American English is the latest major development of Late Modern English, and, as H. L. Mencken never tired of pointing out, it represents a renaissance of its own kind. The American language is somewhat in the position of sixteenth century English in that it is in the process of existing without strong rules. Unlike the language of Beowulf, it borrows from everywhere; like the language of Shakespeare, it is relatively new and lends itself to new forms.

A FINAL GLIMPSE OF DIFFERENCES

The foregoing summary is meant to give you some perspective on the development of the language of *Beowulf* into the complex group of dialects which is called English and which is spoken natively by over a quarter of a billion people (and by millions more as a second language). The final sequence should make the process clearer. The following are the same quotation from nine translations of the Bible, Matthew 5:13:

Old English, 995

Ge synd eorthan sealt; gyf thaet sealt awyrth, on tham the hit gesylt bith? (Literal translation: you are the earth salt; if the salt away - does, with what that it salted is [will be]?)

Wycliffe Gospels, 1389

Yee ben salt of the erthe; that yif the salt shal vanyshe away, wherynne shal it be saltid?

Tyndale Gospels, 1526

Ye are the salt of the erthe; but and if the salt be once vnsavery, what can be salted ther with?

Geneva Bible, 1560

Ye are the salte of the earth: but if the salte haue lost its sauour, wherewith shal it be salted?

Reims (Douai) Bible, 1582

You are the salt of the earth. But if the salt leese his vertue. vvherevvith shall it be salted?

King James, 1611

Yee are the salt of the earth: But if the salt haue lost his sauour. wherewith shal it be salted?

Moffatt Translation, 1922

You are the salt of the earth. But if the salt becomes insipid, what can make it salt again?

You are the salt of the earth; but if the salt has lost its taste, how shall its saltness be restored?

The differences are striking and illustrate something of the way the language developed. Chaucer wrote a different language too, but a small lexicon is all we need to get through. *Beowulf* is another story - and another language. But, as we know, we are not reading *Beowulf* if we do not read Old English.

THE ELEMENTS OF ANGLO-SAXON POETRY

Place in the History of Poetry

We saw above that Modern English descends from a dialect other than the one we read in Old English literature. The term "Old English" therefore serves mainly to establish the continuity of the literature, rather than the language. Prof. C. L. Wrenn (see Bibliography) has shown that there has been a continuity in English literature of the Anglo-Saxon tradition in thought, mood, and subject matter and that, on a technical level, Anglo-Saxon meters (syllabic and stress patterns) have persisted. A student of modern poetry knows of the emphasis that certain poets (notably Ezra Pound: see, for example, his translation of The Seafarer) have placed on Anglo-Saxon rhythms and subject matter. And one need only listen well to a good reading of Anglo-Saxon poems (such as that by Bessinger on record: see Bibliography) to hear a poetic sensibility - a poetic "ear" - that lives on in the poetry of Gerard Manley Hopkins, James Joyce (especially in Ulysses and Finnegan's Wake), Dylan Thomas, T. S. Eliot (especially in the Wasteland), Ezra Pound and others. All of this is by way of saying that Anglo-Saxon is only a "dead" language in the sense that it is not spoken and a "dead" literature in that very few people can read it well enough to realize its rich literary values. Obviously a translation can only bring us the broad outlines of the original and none of the complex nuances of sound and color. As the English poet Coleridge remarked, poetry is that which is lost in translation. (Note: for an example of a close reading of an Anglo-Saxon lyric poem, see our discussion of The Wanderer below.)

THE SCOP

Our earliest literatures in virtually all languages are the product of oral traditions which developed out of the first songs sung and tales told. In the case of Anglo-Saxon literature, these traditions go back to the Germanic tribes which lived on the Continent. The poet was a wandering person, like the Provencal troubadour, the German minnesinger, and the French trouvere, minstrel, and jongleur of the Middle Ages, who went to various courts in search of a patron among the lords. The role of the poet, called a scop (which means literally a "shaper"), was to entertain during celebrations - feasts involving members of the court - and sing heroic tales. Some of the heroes were real and some legendary, but if their names lived on it was largely because they were the subject of the scop. We will see in *Beowulf* the scop who sings at Hrothgar's court of Sigemund (the Volsung) and his heroic defeat of a dragon. But, as we have seen in our glimpse of the Anglo-Saxon people and language, Christianity had a profound influence upon the traditions which came to be expressed in poetry and prose. Thus the Christian scribes turned their attention to what could in some way fit into Christian ideas, and, since all our manuscripts date from about the year 1000, the subject matter of the scop tends away from pagan conceptions of the heroic to the adapted Christian versions.

THE STRUCTURE OF OLD ENGLISH POETRY

The most striking difference between Old and later English poetry is in its technical structure. Every "line" actually consists of two clearly separated half-lines between which is a pause (called a caesura). The two parts are united by **alliteration** - which is really a form of **rhyme**, an initial **rhyme** or "head rhyme." **Alliteration** is conventionally the repetition of consonant sounds, usually at the beginnings of words. However, **alliteration** or initial **rhyme** is interpreted in Old English poetry more broadly than has been the case in later literature, for, in addition to the repetition of similar consonants, it includes the rhyming of any vowel with any other vowel. (Another instance of the continuity of English poetry is the practice of some modern poets to rely heavily on such vowel-rhymes within the line as a way of enriching the particular music of the poem.) Every half-line consists of two "feet" - rhythmic stresses or accents. This "foot" is the basic unit of the poetry. The half-line of two feet has its own metrical pattern (and consequently its own scansion or analysis of the metrical pattern, as we shall see below). There is rarely any end-rhyme in Old English poetry, for the practice of rhyming the final words in the lines was a late development in English poetry. (Once again we should note that modern poetry, like Old English poetry, is often organized by methods other than end-rhyme, notably sound devices occurring within the line.) Generally there are three **alliterations** per line: two in the first half-line and one on the first "foot" of the second half-line. The stressed syllable in the half-line carries the **alliteration**, and usually the third accented syllable sets up the **alliteration**. Let us take a look at lines four and five of *Beowulf* to see a classical example of this alliterative verse:

Oft Scyld Sceafing/sceathena threatum,
monegum maedthum/meodosetla ofteah.

(Oft Scyld Scef's son/from bands of robbers,
from many tribes,/their mead-benches dragged
away.)

The italicized sounds alliterate, two in the first half-line and
one in the second half-line. There are many variations within
the rigidly established pattern, but we cannot fruitfully consider
them here. It will be worth while to glance at the first lines of *The
Seafarer*, the Old English **elegy** which is known widely in Ezra
Pound's version. We include Pound's version, which captures a
good deal of the special music of the Old English but which is at
considerable variance from the original in meaning:

Maeg ic be me sylfum sothgied wrecan,
sithas secgan, hu ic geswincdagum earfothhwile
oft throwade, bitre breostceare gebiden haebbe,
gecunnad in ceole cearselda fela, atol ytha gewealc;
thaer mec oft bigeat nearo nihtwaco aet nacan
stefnan, thonne he be clifum cnossath ...

Pound's version:

May I for my own self song's truth reckon,
Journey's jargon, how I in harsh days
Hardship endured oft.
Bitter breast-cares have I abided,
Known on my keel many a care's hold,
And dire sea-surge, and there I oft spent
Narrow nightwatch nigh; the ship's head
While she tossed close to cliffs ...

We feel in this the rush of the famous "word-horde," - a
kenning for poem - the heavy pounding rhythm (so appropriate
for the subject of severe woes and a rugged existence), the

strong **alliteration**. We feel the force of the seafarer's plight, and his song contains the musical qualities which take us into the experience.

THE KENNING

In addition to the above devices, the scop used a kind of figurative language called the kenning in order to embellish ordinary objects. Like the Homeric epithet (such as "swift-footed Achilles" and "rosy-fingered dawn"), the kenning was a standard phrase or **metaphor** composed of a compound of two words, which became the formula for a specific object: "the leavings of hammers" for swords, the "world-candle" for the sun, "the whale-road" or "sea-monster's home" for the sea, etc. Very often the lesser poet would resort to kennings which had become cliches, such as "ring-giver" for every prince. But the kenning, used with originality, served the purpose of **metaphor**, and, like metaphor, its use was varied and complex.

RHETORICAL TECHNIQUES

Rhetorical techniques are those which alter the particular arrangement of words in order to gain special emphasis. They differ from figurative devices like **metaphors** and kennings in that they do not change the basic meanings of the words used. Thus litotes (a type of meiosis or understatement wherein something is stated as less important than it really is) expresses an idea by denying its opposite. These rhetorical techniques are a form of ironical understatement meant to draw attention to the object. Litotes was a favorite technique by which the Old English poet embellished his subject. For example, in *Beowulf* the poet describes the end of Grendel's bloody career with the words:

"Very different his (Grendel's) fate from that which befell him in earlier days!" In the midst of a grim description of the battle between Beowulf and Grendel, this ironical understatement is an effective device. The poet often elaborated his subject, letting words grow with his awareness of the experience. Again in the Pound translation cited above: "Bitter breast cares have I abided,/ Known on my keel many a care's hold ..." Much poetry coming out of the oral tradition like that of the Bible, *The Iliad*, and *Beowulf*, tends to employ such elaboration as this and tends to make catalogs of the qualities of individuals. For example, Wiglaf is introduced in Canto XXXVI of *Beowulf*: "Wiglaf was called Weohstan's son,/ a beloved shield-warrior, a Scylfings' lord,/ Aelfhere's kinsman..." This piling up of qualities, each of which is a slight variation on the other, is one of the most common rhetorical techniques. We see such variation in the announcement of Beowulf's death in Canto XXXIX:

Now is the kind giver of the Weder's people,
the Goth's lord, fast on his deathbed.
He rests on his deadly couch by the worm's deeds ...

This is restatement for the poetic purpose of establishing the emotional weight of the death.

OTHER TECHNIQUES

We could mention many other techniques, but we shall confine ourselves to suggesting a couple of others. Envelope pattern is a method of organizing a section of a poem (or whole poem) by beginning and ending it with similar statements and rhythms. Thus lines 74 to 110 in The Wanderer form an envelope by beginning with ealre thisse worulde wela westa stondeth ("all the wealth of this world will stand waste") and ending with eal this eorthan gesteal idel weortheth ("the whole state of the world is vain"). The echoes of sound and general meaning allow a figure-like restatement-variation within which there is a dramatic development of related themes. Generative composition, as defined by Rosier (see Bibliography) is "the reuse within a few lines of a given word which is usually in the same class (viz., noun, adjective, etc.) as the original use, and which may or may not have precisely the same meaning or referent." He distinguished between lexical generation, wherein the word itself influences the choice of words which follow, and conceptual generation where it is the "idea" of a word rather than the word itself which attracts or induces other words ... For example, Rosier demonstrates that in *The Wanderer*, which shows the mind of the wanderer as it develops, the words for the mind and its faculties occur throughout the poem - about thirty-five times in 115 lines (mod, the word for mind, occurs eight times either alone or in a combination). It is interesting to reflect on this kind of composition, for it seems to imply that the poet's sensibility attained its focus literally through words. Rosier cogently argues for this method as a basic organizing device in *The Wanderer*, and it has been shown that much of this occurs in *Beowulf*. (See Bibliography for Beaty's "The Echo-Word in *Beowulf*.")

THE BASIS FOR VERSIFICATION

We saw above that the harp found at Sutton Hoo was an important part of the scop's performance. There has been a great deal of speculation about the role of this instrument in Old English versification.

An old theory held that the scop struck his harp at each of the four stresses in the line of poetry. However a more recent and acceptable theory (see Bibliography: John C. Pope, *The Rhythm of Beowulf*) states that the rests often occurring before unaccented syllables probably took the stroke of the harp. To hear a brilliant hypothetical recreation of an Old English poem according to this theory, the student should listen to Prof. Bessinger's record of readings (see Bibliography) where he plays the Sutton Hoo type of harp while singing Caedmon's Hymn. Pope's theory speaks of rhythm in terms of musical analogies. Each line is composed of two half-lines, each half-line of two feet. The half-line is sung (or chanted) in 4/4 or 4/8 time.

THE MANUSCRIPTS OF OLD ENGLISH POETRY

As we have said, most of the Old English poetry in existence - which is a small remnant - comes to us in manuscripts dating from about the year 1000 and written in West Saxon Old English. Many of the originals were written quite a bit earlier, but there is much controversy over the dates. The following are the four principal manuscripts:

1. The *Beowulf* manuscript contains *Beowulf* and *Judith* (the fragment of a religious poem on the Biblical tale: c. 9th century); it is in the Cotton collection of the British Museum.

2. The Junius manuscript contains the Caedmonian poems (religious poems associated with the poet Caedmon, though not written by him; the only poem attributed to Caedmon, the shepherd who was divinely inspired, is the Hymn, found in the Latin manuscripts of Bede's *History*; this poem apparently dates from before 737 - the date of the poem found in the original Northumbrian dialect); it is in the Bodleian Library at Oxford.

3. The Exeter Book contains *Widsith* (see below), riddles, some Cynewulfian poems (religious poems by or ascribed to the poet Cynewulf - the only Old English poet to have signed any manuscript), and elegies (discussed below); it is in Exeter Cathedral.

4. The Vercelli manuscript contains *Andreas* and *A Dream of The Rood* (the former, a religious poem possibly imitative of *Beowulf*; the latter, a religious lyric and one of the great poems of English literature; it is in Vercelli, in Piedmont, Northern Italy.

BEOWULF

. . . .

THE EPIC

The word "**epic**" comes from the Greek meaning "tale." It is a long narrative poem which deals with **themes** and characters of heroic proportions. Its style is exalted. We may conveniently divide **epics** into the two types distinguished by C. S. Lewis. Primary **epics** are the earliest written versions of poems which, at least in part, came out of an oral tradition. Probably the tales were sung by generations of poets and were finally put into written form by a literate poet or a scribe. The greatest primary **epics** known to us are *The Iliad*, *The Odyssey*, and *Beowulf*. Secondary **epics** are later versions which draw some degree of their style and subject matter from earlier epics, and in this class we may include Virgil's *Aeneid*, which took its inspiration from Homer. Other works, which take their direction at least in part from **epics** include: Dante's *Divine Comedy*, Tasso's *Gerusalema Liberata*, Spenser's *Faerie Queen*, and Milton's *Paradise Lost*.

The **conventions** of the **epic**, as established by Homer and Virgil (who, though later than Homer, had a greater influence on literature before the eighteenth century), include: an exalted dignified style; a complex **theme** and narrative which recapitulate the significant preoccupations and experiences of an epoch; a hero who is the epitome of a nation and culture; and a beginning of the narrative in medias res, in the middle of things. There are many other **conventions** which are too complex to discuss here.

BEOWULF AS EPIC

Beowulf, as will be seen when we discuss the poem in detail, embodies these general characteristics in its own special way. The poet concentrates on a section of the life and exploits of a central hero as part of the historical progression of a people, the ideals of which the hero embodies. Similarly, the focus of the *Iliad* is upon Achilles and certain actions during the Trojan War, the *Odyssey* upon Odysseus and his journey, the *Aeneid* upon Aeneas, etc. We do not enter in medias res in the sense of the *Iliad*, but we enter Beowulf's life at a particular time and hear of the historical context into which it fits: Scyld Sceafing and the Scyldings, the struggle between the Danes and the Heathobards, etc. The poem represents the essential elements of the culture in its fusing of pagan and Christian elements. It tells of heroic struggles. And the style is elaborate and exalted in a way which embodies the spirit of its heroic subject.

EARLIER EPICS

Beowulf (c. 650–750) is a relatively late product of Anglo-Saxon civilization, though stylistically, some critics have argued, it represents an earlier stage in the development of oral poetry than do the *Iliad* and the *Odyssey* (see Bibliography for the article by William Whallon). There is some possibility that the *Beowulf* poet was indebted to Virgil, since it embodies many of the characteristics of that poet's work. (For a discussion of this possibility, see Tom Burns Haber, *A Comparative Study of the Beowulf and the Aeneid* [Princeton: Princeton University Press, 1931].) In any case, it is probable that there were fully developed **epics** in Anglo-Saxon before *Beowulf,* some of which may never have been recorded and others of which may have been lost. The qualities of the earliest epics, products of the oral traditions of the so-called heroic age of the Continental Germanic tribes, can perhaps be glimpsed in certain poems and poetic fragments. Among these are *Widsith, Walder,* and *The Fight at Finnsburg.*

WIDSITH

This **epic** is not intended to be the song of a single scop or minstrel but rather recounts the story of all minstrels who wander and glorify great men and their actions. A long list of great heroes is recited in the poem, including Alexander, Caesar, Attila the Hun, Hrothgar (who is a character in *Beowulf*) and Hagen (who appears in The *Nibelungenlied*).

Most scholars feel that *Widsith* is a composite of several lesser pieces and that the poem is not an autobiography. Obviously no minstrel could have visited rulers who were separated by several centuries. The first catalog of kings is of great antiquity, written at least as early as the sixth century. The remainder of the poem was written later and the "autobiographical" lines (see below) last of all. *Widsith*, in the form in which we have it, was put together in the late seventh or early eighth century. The manuscript - from the Exeter Book - is from the late tenth century.

The nature of the poem is clearly exemplified in these "autobiographical" lines:

"I have journeyed over many strange lands in the wide world; I saw goodness and evil, I was separated from my children, I was away from my kindred, but I followed wisely. Thus it is that I can sing and tell a tale, and recount before everyone in the mead-hall how the noble of race treated me well." (lines 101–114)

These lines are perhaps the autobiographical intrusions of a later scop who added to the fragments of *Widsith*. They are not, however, related to other parts. This "word-horde" has more value as a catalog of the principal figures of the heroic age than as poetry.

THE FIGHT AT FINNSBURG (C. 750)

This poem, a fragment of about forty lines, was written at about the same time as *Beowulf*. The subject is a battle between the Frisians, led by King Finn, and the Danes, led by Hnaef. The Danes are treacherously attacked in a mead-hall, in which apparently they are guests, and they fight for five days. At this point the narrative is broken off but we learn from *Beowulf* that a truce is declared after Hnaef is killed. (See The Finnsburg **Episode** in Canto XVI of *Beowulf*.)

WALDERE (C. 750)

This is a poem that survives in two fragments which were, presumably, parts of a longer poem concerning Walther of Aquitaine or Walter of Spain. The first fragment is part of the maiden Hildegund's speech which urges her lover, Walter, to fight the Frankish Warrior, Hagen. The second fragment consists, chiefly, in Walther's reply. These fragments are important because of their relation to the great Volsung-Nibelungen sagas of Germany and Scandinavia.

EPICS AFTER BEOWULF

As late as the tenth century there are representatives of the epic tradition to be found. *The Battle of Brunanburh* is the entry in most of the manuscripts of *the Anglo-Saxon Chronicle* for the year 937. This narrative poem recounts the defeat of a combination of Norsemen and Scots by the Anglo-Saxons under King Athelstan, a successor of King Alfred. *The Battle of Maldon,* however, is a narrative poem which recounts the defeat of the Anglo-Saxons by a contingent of Danes in the year 991. Maldon is fragmentary, although there is not too much missing. In both poems the battle scenes are gruesomely detailed, but they demonstrate the persistence of the institution of comitatus as something which the Anglo-Saxon still revered.

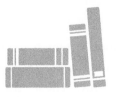

BEOWULF

. . . .

GREAT OLD ENGLISH POEMS

Outside of the heroic traditions of *Beowulf*, there is a body of poetry which stands, in a few instances, amidst the great poetry of English literature. Some of the lyrics (called "elegies"), such as *The Wanderer* and *The Seafarer*, and the religious lyric *A Dream of the Rood* are worth in themselves the pains of learning Anglo-Saxon. It is difficult, perhaps impossible, to find a lyrical poem which rises above these with their finely wrought music and development. Their sophistication in the use of technical devices and their complexity of effects as works of art demonstrate the limitations of an idea of progress in art, for these can hardly be said to run behind later lyrics. The poets' entrance into the language of poetry in order to create there the life of their subjects is dazzling. In addition to the elegiac poetry, there is a significant body of religious poetry, in which is found the great poem, *A Dream of the Rood*. It will help our perspective to survey these poems briefly.

ELEGIAC POEMS

As we noted earlier, the Germanic conception of destiny or fate (wyrd) was a very profound one to the extent that the deity Wyrd became confused with the Christian Almighty God. We shall examine sections in *Beowulf* which demonstrate this paradoxical intermingling of pagan and Christian, but the point is that the Anglo-Saxons regarded life as a struggle by man within his limitations against time, the great destroyer, and the passing glories of this earth. A poem devoted to the illusory and fleeting nature of life is called an **elegy** and to the poems thus written have been given the name elegiac poems. Unlike the poems we usually call "elegies," these poems are not concerned with personal death.

Many fine elegiac lines in *Beowulf* (for example, *The Survivor's Lament*) give evidence that the elegiac tradition is certainly no later than the seventh or eighth century. The Anglo-Saxon's contemplation of the vanished Romano-Briton civilization, or his contemplation of his own dying society may have provided him with some of the melancholic, nostalgic outlook which could be so completely expressed in elegiac verse.

THE WANDERER

We had occasion earlier to have a look at some of *The Seafarer* in the original and in Pound's version. Now let us glance at the other great elegy, *The Wanderer*, which, on the face of it, "realistically" describes the spiritual journey of a wanderer (an eardstapa, meaning "earth-treader"). Now an exile out on the icy seas, he thinks back to the days when he served his lord (in the comitatus relationship), and he has a dream in which he bows to his lord, putting his head in his lord's knees and pledging loyalty.

However his excited imagination is too great for sleep, and he is ripped from bliss and left in the empty, grim, lonely reality of his wandering on the icy sea. He calls to "old comrades" (who, as some critics suggest, are possibly seagulls) but they disappear in the air without a word. Now he laments the loss of his glorious past to the ravages of time in the ubi sunt ("Where are ... ?") **theme** which is so important in medieval literature. (Ubi sunt were the beginning words of many medieval Latin poems, but the lines most familiar to us are those of the medieval French poet Francois Villon in his Ballade: "Where are the snows of yesteryear?" It was translated into English by Dante Gabriel Rossetti as "The **Ballad** of Dead Ladies.") Thus the wanderer asks: "Where now is the warrior? Where is the war-horse?" And he concludes: "... those days have long ago rushed/ Into the night of the past, as if they had never existed!" The wanderer comes to see that "all is wretchedness in the realm of the earth," and he has made his spiritual journey from eardstapa to a man of wisdom (snotter on mode). At the end he has moved into a transcendental Christian reality wherein comfort is possible.

INTERPRETATIONS OF THE WANDERER

There are many different views on the particulars in the poem and at least three widely accepted and very different interpretations: that the wanderer turns to Christian salvation; that the poet, a Christian, uses the wanderer, a pagan, as an object for his dogmatism; that the poem is a Christian allegory, not the account of a real wanderer. But it is clear that the poem is in some sense a **dramatic monologue** - a complete dramatic experience conveyed to us through the words and thoughts of the person who endures it. Yet there is a separation of personae (of the speaking dramatic characters) in that we hear in the beginning, the middle, and the end, the voice of the poet-narrator. Also, the eardstapa himself has different voices, for he is at different stages in his spiritual development at different points in the poem. It seems likely that in half of Part I (which encompasses half of the one-hundred-and-fifteen-line poem) he reflects on his happy past in his own voice but that the narrator seems to enter abruptly to tell of what happens in the subjective experience of the wanderer. We probably actually hear very little of the wanderer's voice.

THE WANDERER AND OTHER OLD ENGLISH POETRY

This shifting about of voices is characteristic of much of Old English elegiac and narrative poetry and could suggest either a special dramatic device or an accumulative method of composition (consistent with the oral tradition) or both. *The Wanderer* thus demonstrates to us some of the ways in which Old English poetry is structured. It poses a Christian world against a pagan world, personal experience against an allegorical use of experience. Unlike most of Anglo-Saxon poetry, The Wanderer is illusive in its presentation of subjective experience; the world of literal experience is seen through the mind and sensibility of the wanderer. Through the voices, **diction**, and special effects of the poem, we enter into his memory, dream, reason, imagination, and the final conceptualizing. In modern terms, we shift from a narrator's monologue to the wanderer's dramatic interior monologue and then to a third-person narrator's voice which takes us through the sensibility - action of the wanderer. (James L. Rosier's article - see Bibliography - gives a brilliant defense of this view and of the view that the poet employed "generative composition" - a method of composition in which the poetry is guided as much by words used, repeated and transformed, as by the experience in the poet's mind. See *The Elements of Old English Poetry* for further discussion.)

OTHER POEMS: THEMES

The very personal sorrow or unhappiness that is found in, for example, *The Husband's Message* or *The Wife's Lament*, is not found in the above-mentioned elegies. In *The Wife*, a woman who has been separated from her husband by captivity voices her bitterness and loneliness:

> **I could deluge the earth with my tears**
> **For grief and parting, for the unresting Heartache of**
> **melancholy ...**

The Husband's Message is less bitter but still pervaded by that personal melancholy of longing. The husband hopes to be reunited with his wife in the springtime, but for the present he "looks longingly":

> **Come to a southbound vessel**
> **And away, on the waves to where**
> **Your husband, your lord, longs for you.**

Another elegiac poem to which the scholars have given great attention is *Wulf* and *Eadwacer*. This is a brief, intense and passionate poem. Some critics have seen this poem as a sketch or fragment of a dramatic monologue. The few lines of *Wulf* treat of a woman who desires her lover, Wulf, and despises her husband, Eadwacer.

CHRISTIAN POEMS

In the writings of Bede we find the story of Caedmon, an illiterate cowherd who was employed by Hild, the abbess of Whitby. As the story goes, Caedmon retired from a banquet and went to sleep when an angel came to him and asked him to sing. In spite of his ignorance and dislike of singing, he sang a short phrase in praise of creating, quoted according to its "general sense" (and not the words) by Bede and now known as Caedmon's Hymn:

Let us give praise to the Maker of heaven's kingdom, the power and end of our Creator, and the deeds of glory's Father. Let us sing how everlasting God, the Worker of all miracles, originally created the skies as a roof to cover the sons of man and how their almighty Protector gave them the earth for their home.

Clearly the poem is little more than a series of epithets applied to God, but its delicate music gives it poetic value. One hears the music in Bessinger's fine recording (see Bibliography). According to Bede, Caedmon composed more lyrics on subjects found in Genesis and Exodus, Christ's Incarnation, and other religious and devotional subjects. Assuming Bede to be correct in his story, then Caedmon is the first poet identified by name in English literature.

CAEDMONIAN POEMS

In the Junius manuscript there are **epic** poems surviving which agree with titles mentioned by Bede: two Genesis poems (A and B), Exodus, Daniel and Christ and Satan. In the Exeter book, the poem *Azarias* is associated with Daniel. These poems, since they were composed by several poets, belong to what is known as the Caedmon "cycle." Between them there are too many differences of style, dialect, and other elements for there to be a possibility that one poet composed them all. The poems of the Caedmon cycle are faithful to all of the scop's traditions, that is, in their use of **alliteration**, kennings, etc. (See Elements of Anglo-Saxon Poetry in this guide.) The Biblical figures assume the place that *Beowulf* assumes in the heroic **epic**. In the poem *Satan* a certain sophistication of outlook is evidenced by the treatment of Satan; that is, a sympathetic examination of his character - for all his evil - which makes that poem a worthy forebear of Milton's *Paradise Lost*. The tendency to moralize imposes severe limitations and extreme unevenness on the poems of the Caedmon cycle but still the poems stand out for their vigorousness and unadornment.

CYNEWULFIAN POEMS

The Cynewulfian poems, which follow the Caedmonian poems in time and literary progression, exhibit a greater church influence than their precursors. These are the first signed poems in English literature. Four of them - *Juliana*, *Elene*, *Christ*, and *The Fates of the Apostles* - have the signature Cyn(e) - wulf written in isolated runic letters. All we know about this Cynewulf is that he was a cleric who lived around the year 800. In *Elene*, the poet's moral condemnation of himself is exaggerated; but after he had passed his youth God gave him the gift of poetry and he has found his happiness. This is a suggestion of the Caedmon myth and indicates a familiarity on the part of the Cynewulfian poets (or at least Cynewulf) with the Caedmonian poems. The Cynewulfian poems have a greater degree of sophistication than even the most sophisticated of the Caedmonian poems (for example, *Satan*). The art of the poet has clearly broken away from some parts of bardic restriction and there is a tendency to less obvious religiosity and moralizing than exists in the Caedmonian poems. It is significant to note that two of the poems have women as their central figures. Other poems which belong to the Cynewulf cycle are *Andreas*, two Guthlac poems, *A Dream of the Rood, The Phoenix, The Harrowing of Hell,* and *The Bestiary* (*Phisiologus*). Scholars have not yet agreed on whether many of the other poems to be found in Old English literature should be included in either the Caedmonian or Cynewulfian cycles. *A Dream of the Rood* is one of the great poems in our literature.

POPULAR LITERATURE

The collection of Riddles - of which there are nearly a hundred in the Exeter book - form much of the body of popular literature. There are also riddles written in Latin which are much the same as their Anglo-Saxon relatives. In general, they picture common objects, phenomena or persons and the reader or listener is left to identify the subject. The liking of primitive peoples for riddles or conundrums is widespread but it may be remarked that many a modern scholar has spent hours in puzzlement over some of the riddles. Popular literature other than the Riddles is varied but a most significant other example is *The Riming Poem*. This is almost the only extant poem in Anglo-Saxon literature which uses end-rhyme as a poetic device: these **rhymes** are antagonistic to the sense of the poem and it has been suggested that this poem is an experiment based upon Latin hymns of the period which used rhyme.

BEOWULF

....

Prose is a later development in civilization than poetry. Old English prose dates from the late ninth, tenth, and eleventh centuries, and its authors are usually known. It is useful to note here the landmarks in the history of prose:

King Alfred the Great (849–899): The "father" of Old English prose, he sought to make Wessex the focal point of culture; in attempting to make the vernacular English the national language, he translated and had translated important Latin texts, including Pope Gregory's *Pastoral Care*, Bede's *Ecclesiastical History*, St. Augustine's *Soliloquies*, Boethius' *Consolation of Philosophy*, and Orosiux' *Universal History*. These had a great effect on the development of later writers.

The Anglo-Saxon Chronicle (891): Discussed above, this document - also called *Old English Annals* - was set up by Alfred and is one of the primary sources for our historical study of England. It covers the period from 55 B.C. (Caesar's first invasion) to 1154 (the accession of Henry II).

Aelfric (c. 955–c. 1020): Abbott Aelfric, of Winchester and Oxfordshire, was the first truly accomplished prose writer in English. His purpose was to instruct those who did not read Latin in the principles of Christian life. His important works are his 120 Homilies (a homily is a work which urges its readers to accept a specific moral view) and his translation of the first seven books of the Bible.

Wulfstan (died 1023): Bishop of London and then of Worcester, Archbishop of York, he also had significant diplomatic and literary careers. He is best remembered for his homilies in which his prose style is accomplished and varied, employing at times such poetic techniques as **rhyme** and alliteration.

Latin Prose: Latin prose naturally flourished throughout the Old and Middle English periods. Most of it was **didactic** and of little literary value. The masterpiece of Anglo-Latin literature is Bede's *Historia Ecclesiastica Gentis Anglorum* (*The Ecclesiastical History of the English People*), discussed above. Other Anglo-Latin writers of note were: Alcuin (735–804) - author of commentary on Genesis; Aldhelm (c. 640–709) - writer of Latin verse and prose; Gildas (c. 516–c. 570) - historian; Nennius (late 8th century) - historian; Asser (died c. 909) - author of a biography of Alfred.

BEOWULF

. . . .

UNITY

Although there is a considerable minority of dissenting opinions, it is generally agreed that *Beowulf* is a unified work, that is, a work whose elements are related to each other in such a way that the meaning of the work is derived from a consideration of the configuration or total configuration of these elements. To the modern reader, this unity may not seem perfectly obvious. In reading *Beowulf* we shall see a number of digressions made by the poet into genealogy and contemporary myth, obscure historical references, repetition of events, and unevenness of time. All of these things, by modern standards, are not always conducive to what Edgar Allen Poe called "unity of effect."

But the difficulties do not lie completely within the poem itself. Obviously the modern reader demands and expects something according to quite different tastes than the eighth-century Anglo-Saxon, and, historically speaking, the modern reader - even if extremely well-read - will encounter difficulties in placing *Beowulf* into a proper historical context. For the Anglo-Saxon audience, the historical digressions of *Beowulf* served to unify the **epic** with facts which were common knowledge (at least to the educated). Without a knowledge of the historical references, of course, much of the **irony** of *Beowulf* is lost. Secondly, the modern reader may not be quite so interested in the telling and retelling of Beowulf's exploits. Once would seem to be enough for a reader (or listener) interested in more subtle psychological motives for these actions. But the actions of Beowulf, his deeds and feats of glory, provide the chief source of interest to the Anglo-Saxon audience. *Beowulf* is addressed largely to the educated class of Anglo-Saxon society, but it must be remembered that this society was "newly settled," and not completely won away from its traditions of warlike spirit, aggressiveness, and the glories of battle. Indeed, the mood of melancholy, harking back to the "days of yore," prevails in much of *Beowulf.*

TRADITIONS

Another puzzling aspect of *Beowulf* to the logical-minded modern reader is the contradiction between elements of Germanic folklore interwoven with Christian morality and Biblical history. As we shall see, Beowulf alternately places his faith in wyrd (fate, or destiny) and the Lord God. Beowulf remarks that "fate goes ever as it must," and the implication is that man is not a creature possessed of much free will, but rather a creature largely at the mercy of higher forces who generally use him as they will. Close to his death, Beowulf remarks that he has "endured his destiny." This is the Stoic resignation of a great warrior: within his limits he has done what he can. But we shall see that the "Lord God triumphant" awards Beowulf the victory over Grendel's mother, the she-monster. The poet will inform us that the Danes need expect no relief from the scourges of Grendel because they have fallen away from the true God. Both Hrothgar and Hygelac give thanks to God for Beowulf's heroic victories over the monsters and Beowulf himself - on the point of dying - gives thanks to God that he has never taken life a kinsman.

It has been argued by critics that *Beowulf* was originally a pagan poem into which elements of Christian tradition and morality were interpolated. Modern scholarship has demonstrated, however, that the Christian elements are so pervasive of Beowulf - down to the **imagery** and language - that they represent no interpolation. Rather, the contradiction must be found in the society itself from which *Beowulf* emerged. The conversion of the Anglo-Saxons took place only a century and a half prior to the composition of *Beowulf* and although its author was quite familiar with the Bible (which supposes that his audience was equally familiar), the Germanic traditions continued to persist. The poet himself has difficulty in deducing the genealogy of Grendel (a Germanic monster) from Cain, the "first murderer." Wyrd, the Germanic deity of fate and destiny, is identified with the Lord God, specifically the Old Testament God, who is a jealous and vengeful god. If, as it has been argued, a Christian society is the antithesis of a military society, then it would be difficult to imagine how the poet could interpolate any New Testament virtues into *Beowulf.* The Old Testament accounts of creation, the flood, Adam and Eve, Cain and Abel, etc., would, of course, be accessible to the Anglo-Saxon apprehension. Not so easy, however, is a "turn-the-other-cheek" morality, or a parable of wheat and tares. Significantly, the poet - perhaps unconsciously - identifies the Christian virtues specifically with women. We shall see in Wealhtheow - the queen of Hrothgar - that she is a "peacemaker" (a role assigned to women, generally, in Anglo-Saxon court circles) and that in her speeches, she talks of honesty, friendship and gentleness. The Christian sin of Pride is treated at length in Hrothgar's discourse, and the vanities of the world are taken up in the brief **episode**, *The Survivor's Lament*. Other New Testament **themes** are touched upon, but never in a directly identifiable way (as in the sense that Lazarus would be mentioned, like Cain), which implies the gradual effusion of Christian morality into the categories of Anglo-Saxon thought. St. Augustine was ordered to proceed slowly with his conversion of Britain and it is as if his task and the task of his successors was to carefully pour new wine into the old bottles.

DIVISIONS

Beowulf must be regarded as one regards the **epic** of Achilles - that is, with respect to the larger context of historical time and place. The life of Beowulf in the **epic** has been seen by some critics as dividing it into two parts: the youthful Beowulf and the old Beowulf. The youthful Beowulf represents a hero without reputation, a young man anxious to do great deeds and behave according to his sense of "form." He is ambitious, somewhat vainglorious, but generous and honest and not an oppressor of the weak. The old Beowulf represents a man slightly weary of the struggles he has outlived, melancholy and contemplative but still possessed of the heroic spark to action, a good king to his people, a shepherd of his flock. While these two appearances of Beowulf may seem contradictory, the divisions are not absolute. We shall see that one of the chief devices providing unity to *Beowulf* is the poet's almost tumultuous references to times present, past and contemporary. The early cantos of *Beowulf* imply events that will happen in later cantos; later cantos refer back to earlier happenings; and by way of digression, contemporaneous historical events are discussed and indicated. This is what one critic called "Beowulf's forward, backward and sideways movement" in time.

Another interpretation divides the **epic** into three parts: Part I, Beowulf's struggle with Grendel; Part II, Beowulf's struggle with Grendel's mother; and Part III, Beowulf's struggle with the dragon. This focus on the three struggles of Beowulf, of course, easily lends itself to allegorical interpretations of Beowulf (if it were not suggested by them). In one sense, the struggles take the form of a "linear" development of the struggle between Good and Evil. We shall see that the monsters become progressively less susceptible to human apprehension (for example, compare Grendel's hand-to-hand struggle with Beowulf to the Dragon's battle) and that they take on more unreal, abstractly identifiable qualities. In another sense, critics have taken the three struggles to represent parables of history. After the deaths of Grendel and his mother and also after the death of the Dragon, the poet mentions portents of decay and doom for both the Spear-Danes and the Geats. The monsters may represent the objectification of internal revolutions or external political enemies (as some critics have contended) which finally will undo these nations as all nations have been undone on earth.

BEOWULF'S ETHIC

In *Beowulf* runs the **theme** of lof, a nearly untranslatable word which means the praise and esteem of one's countrymen and contemporaries. A statement of this appears at the very beginning of *Beowulf*: "For among all peoples it is only through those actions which merit praise that a man may prosper." Fame, contends the poet, is the most permanent of all things in an impermanent world. Of all that a man can have, fame survives everything of the transient and unstable. Modern philosophy might render lof as "objective immortality," in the sense that one's existence depends on someone knowing it. Throughout the poem Beowulf is described as a man "hungry for fame," and the final eulogy praises Beowulf as "most desirous of reknown." Contrasted with this is the statement of Wiglaf that death is better than dishonor.

The idea of the illusory nature of the world is a favorite subject of Old English literature. To the Anglo-Saxon conception of the warrior's struggles against the ebbing tides of life must be added the Christian other-worldliness to arrive at this particular admixture of "days of yore," and "veil of illusion." A good example of this melancholic sentiment occurs in *The Seafarer*:

The wealth
Of the world neither reaches to heaven nor remains.
No man has ever faced the dawn
Certain which of Fate's three threats
Would fall; illness, or age, or an enemy's
Sword, snatching the life from his soul.

Closely allied to the sentimental view of a transient and impermanent universe is the concept of wyrd (fate or destiny, as mentioned earlier). The God Wyrd stands behind the world of appearances decreeing the vicissitudes of a man's life and against whom man's power and knowledge do not avail. The sermon of Hrothgar on pride - man's sin of reposing in the illusion of knowledge, or the illusion of his own powers - touches on what the Greeks might have called hybris, a pride not unlike Christian pride but implying also that man has presumed upon the will of the gods. Pride, as it occurs in *Beowulf*, signifies the arrogation of a faith to one's self that belongs rightfully to Wyrd or God. Hrothgar comments that for the prideful man "... the world turns at his will; he does not know better." Hrothgar's sermon shows us also that no matter how much a man may have, in terms of wealth or power, he will depart the earth sadly and disillusioned, reminding us of a statement by Aeschylus: "Who sows the seeds of pride, reaps a harvest of tears."

The thoughtful reader may ask, then, what sustaining force is there behind the pessimistic consideration of man's impotence against a blind and impersonal fate? The question has been posed many times by the poet of *Beowulf* and it is Beowulf himself who provides the answer. Beowulf believes that a man must depend on the tiny amount of free will at his disposal: he must make the right choices when he can, and then: "... unless a man is doomed beforehand, fate is likely to be favorable to the courageous ..." Thus free will is equated with courage and the courageous man - one who is able to do deeds in the face of the world - will achieve fame (lof) which is the only thing worth having. This concept may be difficult for the modern reader to accept because of the prevalence of such words as "individualism," "freedom," etc., in our vocabulary. As we have seen, however, the Anglo-Saxon conception of freedom was much more limited than hours and involved itself with a man's courage, his ability to make the right or good choice in the face of the world.

BEOWULF

. . . .

PROLOGUE

Beowulf opens with a genealogy of the royal house of the Spear-Danes, beginning with Scyld Sceafing, "Scyld, son of Sceaf." Scyld, who we are informed started his life as a foundling or castaway, later attained the heights of power and empire. The tendency to obscure the origins of Scyld is a mythical device which is paralleled (as we remember) in the myth of Moses and ironically in the myth of Oedipus. This obscurity renders a character more symbolical or general in a sense and is found in modern fictional works, an example of which is Melville's *Billy Budd*.

Scyld however "was a good king" and it is fitting that his son Beowulf – not the Beowulf of this **epic** - should win fame throughout Scandinavia. "It is fitting," we are advised, "that a son should merit the honor of his father's comrades," a sentiment not uncommonly found in societies where the patriarchal family is the fundamental unit. The poem concludes its account of the eponymous Scyld with his death and funeral:

> At his destined hour, Scyld, the great striver,
> departed to go into the protection of the Lord.

Appropriately Scyld is borne away on the sea and we remember that as a child he was borne on the sea to Denmark. It is as if Scyld were regarded as a child of the ocean, the ocean symbolizing the future and primordial time. We are reminded of Tennyson's phrase which he applies to Arthur (who is of equally obscure origins): "from deep to deep he goes."

As we shall see later, an underlying motif in the introduction is the rise and fall of nations and the suggestion of earlier times which are wrapped in the veil of the mysterious. Significantly, the poet does not begin his account of Beowulf in medias res (as Homer began the *Iliad*) but rather refers in the first lines to "days of yore," that is, to a time when heroes and demigods walked the earth. Critics have taken reference of this sort (the Scyld **episode**) as a sort of paradoxical persistence of Anglo-Saxon tradition alongside an incipient Christian tradition. We shall see many more examples of this later in *Beowulf*.

CANTO I

After the death and funeral of Scyld Sceafing, his son Beowulf ruled the Spear-Danes for a long time, and subsequently the "lofty Healfdene," Beowulf's son, became ruler. From Healfdene sprang four children, three of whom are named: Heorogar, Hrothgar and Halga. Hrothgar achieved glory and fame in war. It was his ambition to command a great mead-hall (a symbol or emblem of prowess in war and the obligation of a lord to his thanes) and his object was attained: "In time it happened, early in his life, that it (the mead-hall) was constructed, of hall-houses the greatest." The name of the great mead-hall was Heorot, a name given it by Hrothgar himself. With the building of the great hall, Hrothgar pledged happiness and security to his subjects and the kingdom settled down to peace and the enjoyment of listening to tales of the bards. The bards, called scops, sang of former times, back to the beginning of time when "the Almighty wrought the earth." The account of the creation in the book of Genesis is referred to in the singing of the "gleemen."

The peace and contentment of Hrothgar and his subjects was not to be permanent, however, because of a "fiend in Hell," who, angered by the singing of the bards, began to perpetrate crimes. Grendel, the "grim guest," is the monster who has descended from Cain, the first murderer, and who spreads evil and destruction wherever he goes.

Comment

Although there is no actual evidence for the existence of Scyld and his son Beowulf, the later Scyldings were apparently a dynasty ruling Denmark from around 550 to 650. Although the Sutton Hoo discovery has confirmed what may seem to be the fancies of the poet concerning the funeral of Scyld, there has been, as yet, no evidence that any of the Anglo-Saxon kings lived in such a hall as Heorot. The name "Heorot" signifies royalty and is derived from the word "Hart," meaning ringlike or regal. The incidents in Heorot indicate that the lord-thane relationship (the comitatus of Tacitus) is preserved and the relationship is clearly delineated. Hrothgar, the "ring-giver," distributes rewards and his faithful thanes expect such gifts in exchange for their services. It was the great shame of a lord (as noted earlier) should he ever be surpassed in valor by one of his thanes and it was their great shame should they ever leave him on the battlefield.

The scop (minstrel or gleeman) entertains the feasting and mead-drinking warriors with songs accompanied by a harp. The poet hints of the destruction of Heorot, however, in the midst of his description of its beauty: "The hall towered high, curving like the horn: great heat from enemy fire awaited it." The hostile fire will either be spread by Grendel, a half-Germanic, half-Christian monster or may be taken as an historical reference - that is, to a future time when Hrothgar's kingdom shall have been destroyed.

CANTO II

Grendel, enraged at the revelry at Heorot, invades the mead-hall and snatches up thirty of the sleeping warriors. He devours the warriors whole and returns again the following evening. The fear inspired by Grendel's monstrous outrage is mentioned ironically by the poet: "Then another place was found by those who would sleep better." The war between the Danes and Grendel continues for twelve unremitting years. There is to be no peace between Grendel and the Danes, and he can be neither defeated nor bought off. The Danes invoked their ancient deities, and the poet mentions that the Danes were, at that time, not aware of the Christian God: "... they did not know the Creator, the Judge of actions, they did not know the Lord God..." And it is suggested that "woe befalls" him who does not pray to the Christian God: "Do not let him to expect comfort nor anything to aid him. Goodwill go to him who, after his death, seeks the Lord ..."

Comment

In this canto a contradiction is found between the monotheistic Christian beliefs presumed in earlier cantos and the deliberate statement that the Danes did not know the "Lord God." Historically, this may refer to a time when the Danes backslid or fell away from the church, as did the Israelites during Moses' ascent upon the mountain fall away from their faith. Alternately, and in line with other unsolved cruces, the passage may represent the persistence of Germanic tradition for those who either had not fully accepted the Christian dogma or for those who had not accepted it at all. In spite of all interpretations, however, a Christian moral is indicated because, as the poet points out, no help shall be given to him who does not pray to the Lord God.

So great was the fear and misery of the Danes that is was openly sung of in song, we are informed. It is through these songs that news will reach Beowulf and he will decide to come to the rescue of Hrothgar.

CANTO III

When Beowulf, thane of Hygelac, hears of Hrothgar's misfortune, he decides to come to his aid. (Beowulf is not an Anglo-Saxon but a member of the Geats - a related Scandinavian people.) We shall see later that a special tie of friendship binds Hrothgar and the father of Beowulf, Ecgtheow. Beowulf's journey over the sea is brilliantly rendered by the poet:

Impelled over the waves by wind The foamy prow like a bird Sped onward till the next day's hour Showed ocean shores shining, lofty hills, Expansive shorelands.

Beowulf and his heroic followers are greeted by a Danish coast-guardsman who does not immediately recognize them. He asks them sternly but politely to identify themselves. In posing this question, the coast-guardsman gives an indication of his function: "For this I am placed at the extremity of land, that no enemies of the Danes may beach their ship-armies." Clearly, the guardsman is impressed with the noble appearance of Beowulf and his retainers. He remarks that he has never seen a "greater earl on earth." Still, it will be necessary for Beowulf to identify himself and explain his mission.

Comment

The old English poets are at their best in describing the sea and journeyings over the sea - the passage here is no exception. The images of the sea in this section of *Beowulf* are suggestive of images that appear in the elegiac poem, *The Seafarer*, bereft, of course, of the element of dread which could not, according to the heroic tradition, appear in the minds of Beowulf or his comrades.

Because of the abundance of petty kingdoms, warlike clans and tribes, and sea-riders of all descriptions, it was the custom of the Danes (as well as most coastal dwellers) to station "coastal guards" who could give alarm in case of any invasion by a raiding party or army. Significantly, the character of the sea-raiders' strategy is rendered obvious by the term "sea-army." The raiders were both soldiers and sailors. We remember from Roman history that in the first Punic war the sea-army of the Romans defeated the superior seamanship of the Carthaginian navy, and so this type of strategy is not really new to military history.

The appearance of Beowulf is impressive to the coast-guardsman and we may contrast the young Beowulf here with the old Beowulf as he shall appear later. As a young man, Beowulf is seen to be vigorous, somewhat vain, aggressive, noble and good. Some of these qualities will become ripened through maturity (as we shall see) but some will become obscured entirely by his subsequent melancholy. Note that the Anglo-Saxon conception of lof or desire for worldly fame makes these characteristics typical of heroes.

CANTO IV

Beowulf identifies himself as a follower of Hygelac and as a member of the Geats. His father is Ecgtheow who is well known to every sage and minstrel. Through kind feeling of Hrothgar, Beowulf says, he seeks to defend him and show him how the foe may be overcome. The guardsman directs them on to Hrothgar and promises that their ship will be defended. From Beowulf's noble words and bearing the guardsman perceives that he is no enemy of the Danes.

Comment

Beowulf makes reference to his famous father and also to a bond that exists between himself (through his father) and Hrothgar, referred to as Healfdene's son. The implication is that Ecgtheow and Hrothgar knew each other earlier.

The function of the coast-guardsman is, in addition to watching for sea-raiders or "sea-armies," to defend friendly ships against despoilment. As Beowulf is a noble hero, and his companions are mighty warriors, so also is the character of his ship once again denoted: "... your ship, newly tarred ..." It will be remembered from Canto III that a "wave traverser good" was prepared for Beowulf's journey and the noble ship is not without the significance, in terms of the **epic**, that would be attached to Jason's *Argo*, or, to cite a variation, Arthur's sword, Excalibur. The point is that the implements or possessions of a hero become imbued with an almost miraculous or holy significance.

CANTO V

After walking up a stone paved road, Beowulf and his band arrive at Heorot. The bearing and dress of the group are impressive and Hrothgar's servant and messenger exclaims: "I have never seen strangers or men any prouder." Beowulf identifies himself again and requests an audience with Hrothgar.

A noble Wendel, Wulfgar, tells him that he will advise Hrothgar who they are and of their mission and will return with Hrothgar's answer. Wulfgar is valorous and wise and "he knew the usage of a court." His function is probably that of court chamberlain in addition to being Hrothgar's advisor. He suggests to Hrothgar that the visitors be granted an audience because they appear to be worthy men, especially their chief, Beowulf.

Comment

That the Danish court is more than a collection of ill-mannered warriors is obvious here. There is a definite court "usage" or etiquette and a sense of "form" is manifest. The proud bearing of Beowulf and his band at first seems to presume upon the honor of the court and it requires the services of the court-wise Wulfgar as intermediary to see that the dignity of neither Hrothgar's court nor his visitors is offended.

CANTO VI

Hrothgar remembers Beowulf as a child and mentions Beowulf's father, Ecgtheow, with some detailed knowledge. He is given hope by the arrival of Beowulf because he knows him to be of noble parentage. Hrothgar offers treasure to Beowulf and his warriors if they are able to rid his land of the monster. Beowulf hails Hrothgar and in grandiose terms delineates his errand to rid the land of the Grendel monster, and to make Heorot useful once again. Beowulf recites that he avenged the Weders' quarrels and petitions that he shall have the honor of challenging the monster and purifying Heorot. For his part, Beowulf says, he will trust in the "Lord's doom," and will bear neither shield nor spear. If the monster triumphs, he continues, then it shall only be through his death and he will have no need to hide is head. Beowulf closes his petition with the mention of wyrd, implacable fate: "Fate goes ever as it must."

Comment

Hrothgar's intimate knowledge of Beowulf's father has been suggested earlier by Beowulf's own statements. On the basis of this knowledge, Hrothgar has asked that Wulfgar welcome Beowulf and his followers. Thus the suggestion of the introductory canto, that is, that a father's son "should merit the honor of his father's comrades," is shown to be true of Beowulf. In the Germanic tradition Beowulf does not understate what his deeds have been or what he intends to do. Speaking to Hrothgar, Beowulf says that, since Grendel does not use weapons, he also disdains them. Continuing, Beowulf mentions his "qualifications" for battling Grendel: he has wrestled victoriously with sea-monsters. Here we see Beowulf as almost pure hero in the tradition of Achilles: proud, disdainful and ambitious.

CANTO VII

Hrothgar continues his reminiscences about Beowulf's father and recounts Ecgtheow's great feat of killing Heatholaf, interweaving an account of his own quarrels with the Wylfings. Abruptly, Hrothgar's conversation changes to the subject of his own present sorrows and tribulations, for which the monster Grendel is directly the cause. In his old age, Hrothgar says, he has seen his mead-hall deprived of retainers and warriors and Heorot is now useless. Hrothgar then invites Beowulf to speak what is on his mind and to partake in the feasting and mead-drinking. Beowulf, his band, and the Danes sit down to drinking and listening to the songs of the scops.

Comment

Hrothgar's discursive rambling may be interpreted as a clever device of the poet to demonstrate Hrothgar's senility (he is referred to in Canto V as "old and hoary"). Most probably, however, the side references pertain to epics or tales well-known to the listeners or readers of *Beowulf* and serve to unify the poem with other elements in Germanic folklore. This method of side references or digressions to contemporaneous tales is manifestly obvious in works of the middle ages as a deliberate literary device. Such works as Eschenbach's Parzifal abound with them. (The interrelation of characters in the works of a single author is the latest development of this device and is seen in the works of such authors as Leo Tolstoy and James Joyce.)

Hrothgar invites Beowulf to sit down with his own warriors "and unbind with mead thy valiant breast..." This is at once an invitation to recount his own deeds of valor publicly in the form of a traditional Germanic beot or boast. This will be a public proclamation of the deeds Beowulf will undertake and as such may be thought of as providing an actual "contract" between Beowulf and Hrothgar.

CANTOS VIII AND IX

During the feast, Beowulf is taunted by Unferth who is jealous of his glory. Unferth asks Beowulf if he is the same one who was bested by Breca, chief of the Brondings, in a swimming contest. Breca, contends Unferth, had more strength than Beowulf and dares Beowulf to spend a night in Heorot. Beowulf replies with a different account of the contest with Breca. Theirs was a youthful venture, Beowulf contends: "When we were younger we agreed and promised (we were both youths) that we should venture our lives upon the ocean ..." Beowulf recounts that they had only swords to defend themselves against the sea-monsters and that they swam together for five nights in icy waters before they become parted. Beowulf was attacked by a monster who dragged him to the bottom of the sea and was killed by Beowulf's own hand. Subsequently, Beowulf describes how he killed nine monsters. Then, overcome with fatigue, he was borne by the sea to the land of the Finns. Breca, Beowulf contends, never achieved a feat equal to this. Beowulf taunts Unferth with the murder of his brothers and says that for these crimes Unferth shall suffer in Hell. Further Beowulf contends that Grendel has no fear of the Spear-Danes and he boasts that a Geat shall overcome the monster. The traditional Germanic beot (warrior's boast, mentioned earlier) is given by Beowulf: "I shall perform deeds of noble valor or meet my end in this very hall." Wealhtheow, Hrothgar's queen, now appears and gives the cup to her husband and then to his retainers. At last she takes the cup to Beowulf and thanks God that he has arrived to save them. She has trust in him, she says. "She thanked God ... that the power to trust in any warrior had overtaken her, for succor against crimes." Beowulf takes the cup and restates the pledge he took when he started upon his journey.

His words please Wealhtheow, and the retainers and people rejoice. Abruptly, Hrothgar rises to make a speech before retiring. He affirms his trust in Beowulf, asks him to be mindful of glory and show his valor. Never before has he turned command of Heorot over to anyone else, he says. Hrothgar promises that: "... for you there shall be no dearth of desirable things, if you escape with your life from this deed of valor."

Comment

The character of Unferth is somewhat contradictory. He is described as jealous and sarcastic and to him is imputed the most heinous of all crimes, fratricide. Later, as we shall note, Beowulf accepts the sword called Hrunting generously offered him by Unferth for use against Grendel's mother. Unferth is a thyle, that is, roughly, an orator or spokesman of Hrothgar, although it seems that his role is more that of inciting the warriors to a great pitch of boasting. His personality is not unlike that of the spidery Thersites in the Iliad, a character whose function is to make thrusts against Ulysses and the other heroes.

As we have seen, Unferth does incite Beowulf to recount the Breca episode (Breca, incidentally, is mentioned in the poem Widsith) and we are given further evidences of Beowulf's valor and prowess. It is significant in terms of Beowulf's reputation that the Breca **Episode** is veiled in obscurity, for we shall see that Beowulf - to his contemporaries - does not yet possess a great reputation; in fact in his homeland just the contrary is true. The Danes, however, are well pleased with Beowulf when the festivities end. The respect accorded Beowulf is clearly evidenced in the statement made by Wealhtheow, and her statements may also be indicative of a certain tendency to idealize the woman and possibly, therefore, her character harks forward to later in the middle ages and the conception of "romantic love."

CANTO X

Hrothgar and his warriors then depart from the hall, leaving Beowulf and his comrades to await the monster. Beowulf removes his armor and sword, handing his equipment to an attendant with a repetition of the boast that he will meet the monster unarmed: "I do not regard myself less powerful in strength or warlike deeds than Grendel does himself." Beowulf's companions are not so assured of the outcome of the battle as their confident leader, however, because as the poet relates: "Not one of them thought he would ever be seeking his homeland again." Beowulf lies down to an (apparently) untroubled sleep, a distinct contrast to his fearful comrades. "From afar in the murky night," Grendel, referred to as the "shadow walker," approaches.

Comment

It is interesting to note the contrast between the boastful, confident Beowulf and his hitherto proud companions who have become more like ordinary men. In this, as in previous sections, the nearer in time we are carried to the appearance of Grendel, that foul monster from the reaches of Hell itself, the more purely heroic does the character of Beowulf become and the greater the contrast between him and those around him. In Beowulf's reply to the Danes, he contrasts the impotent Danes with a "man of the Geats," and now we see the transcendence of Beowulf - in heroic proportions - even to men of his own tribe.

Beowulf's companions are thinking about home, their families and "free city," possibly lamenting the fact that they ever undertook the journey. Beowulf, on the contrary, only thinks of the glory and settles down to sleep. This contrast creates a great deal of tension - especially considering the beliefs of the Anglo-Saxon mind at this period - because of the fearful men, the unconcerned hero, and the monster lurking from afar. It is Beowulf's faith in wyrd (fate or destiny) that seemingly has transformed itself into a faith in God: "It has been truly demonstrated that Almighty God rules the race of men." This statement, however, made by the poet himself as an observation (typical of the poet's entrances into the poetry), is well in keeping with statements made by Beowulf later and demonstrates Beowulf's (as well as the Anglo-Saxon) alternate faith in Wyrd and God. It is Beowulf's faith in Wyrd - God that lends to him credence as a character and that will resolve his apparent lack of concern with the power of Grendel or loss of his own life. This, of course, is not to be confused with Beowulf's courage, the positive manifestation of his faith.

CANTO XI

Grendel comes stalking from the moor, smashes down the door of Heorot with "fire-hard hands" and stands amidst the sleeping warriors with a horrid flame standing from his eyes. From the "kindred band of sleeping warriors" Grendel snatches one man and devours him. Grendel reaches toward Beowulf and finds himself enmeshed in the warrior's stronger grip. Grendel becomes fearful and longs to flee but Beowulf does not remit his grasp. The monster struggles fearfully to escape and the hall can barely stand the reverberations of the terrible struggle. Outside the Danes are terrified by the awesomeness of Grendel's wailings.

Comment

In this canto Grendel appears as an incarnation of Satan himself. He is described as "a wicked spoiler of men," "the fiend," and one with "fire-hard hands," "from whose eye a horrid flame stood." Further, he is referred to as a "miserable wight," "a fell wretch," and "the criminal." Thus, we should not be more hesitant in regarding Grendel as Satan himself - based on these terms - than the original listeners. The origins of Grendel are equally as allusive of the Christian Satan and Christian Hell. Grendel comes "stalking from the moor," a mysterious region where, it was mentioned earlier, the unbaptized dare not enter. Grendel is a creature of night, a "shadow walker," and his place of habitation is in the mid-earth of the world's regions. The "fire-hard hands," and the "horrid light" all may refer indirectly to the fires of Hell. Significantly, Grendel wishes to escape Beowulf's grip and retreat to his subterranean cavern but cannot.

Beowulf himself, however, does not escape from the abundance of fearful **imagery** cast over the monster. The angry Beowulf is one of "the warlike beasts," he is one of the "fierce ones," and it is suggested that the wrath of Beowulf is no less terrible to behold than the lust of the "pernicious spoiler." Finally, Canto XI closes with the monster's wail of defeat, which terrorizes the Danes. This forms an effective contrast to the voice of God heard at the beginning of time and of the Word which was heard even to the bottom of the abyss. The mournful shriek of Grendel may be taken as the shrieking of Satan himself, symbolizing his defeat and the fact that he is bound to Hell forever.

CANTO XII

The companions of Beowulf, awakened by the struggle, rally to defend their lord but their swords are useless against the monster because he has cast a spell on them. Finally, Grendel tears his arm out of his socket in his struggle to be free and the creature runs screaming in pain and terror into the night. Grendel returns to the fens, knowing that he is dying. When Beowulf sees that Grendel is vanquished and fleeing, he celebrates and rejoices in his valor and glories. Beowulf fastens Grendel's arm (which had been left behind) high up on the wall of the mead-hall.

Comment

The struggle between Beowulf and Grendel is an intensely personal struggle in which neither of the combatants uses arms. It is almost as if it were a struggle between the wills of the adversaries themselves. Significantly, Beowulf's comrades are able to offer him no aid and their swords are useless against the monster. Beowulf is satisfied to know that he has triumphed and leaves it up to his comrades to follow the trail of the monster's blood.

CANTO XIII

The warriors of the Danes gather from far and near on the next morning to view the trophy and praise the valor of Beowulf.

Hrothgar is also praised as a good king. The exploits of Beowulf are sung and a tale from *the Nibelungenlied* is introduced concerning Sigemund who destroyed a great dragon and thereby gained a great treasure. There follows a tale about King Heremod, presumably of the dynasty preceding the Scyldings. When this is concluded all return to Heorot to view the trophy and there Hrothgar is joined by Wealhtheow and her maidens.

Comment

In the true Germanic tradition, the great victory is followed by feasting and celebrating, and songs are sung about the great deeds of heroes. The story of Sigemund may seem to be out of place here but it must be remembered that such digressions served to make Beowulf more real to its listeners or readers, who would naturally be more familiar with such references than the modern student. Also the **episode** has parallels with Beowulf.

CANTO XIV

Hrothgar goes into Heorot and looks at the arm of the monster which Beowulf has nailed up. He speaks about the misery and grief brought to his kingdom by Grendel and of the great feat of valor performed by Beowulf. Hrothgar tells Beowulf that hereafter he will love him as a son and that Beowulf will not lack "of desirable worldly things /that I have power over." Beowulf then describes his conflict with the monster and states that the creature will surely find great doom from the Almighty Creator. Unferth (Ecglaf's son) is silent as all affirm that no sword or weapon could equal the feat performed by Beowulf with his bare hands.

Comment

in Hrothgar's speech, thanks is given to the Almighty and recalls the words of the poet before the appearance of the monster: "It is truly shown that Almighty God rules the race of men." Hrothgar, as evidence of his great feeling for Beowulf, offers a reward greater than even all the gold and treasures which will also be given: he takes Beowulf into the bonds of kinship as a son.

Beowulf is more modest in this section than when he had undertaken his beot (boast) of his great accomplishments and promises. His account of the battle with Grendel is given simply and parallels the account given earlier in the poem. Significantly, we do not hear from Unferth as he views the monster's arm and nails of "steel."

CANTO XV

It is ordered that Heorot be cleansed, repaired and decorated for the feast that will follow. Golden tapestries are hung on the walls and food and drink in plenty are provided. Hrothgar presents Beowulf with a banner, a breastplate and helmet. After Beowulf drinks the health of Hrothgar, he is presented with eight stallions and eight jeweled saddles to be added to his gifts. One of the saddles, inlaid and adorned with jewels, is Hrothgar's own which he rode to war.

Comment

As we have mentioned, the giving of gifts from lord to thane was the accepted (and commonly expected) practice and formed part of the institution of comitatus. Beowulf, of course, has undertaken to defeat Grendel partly because of Hrothgar's bond with Ecgtheow and partly because Beowulf seeks fame. As an exception to court procedure and "usage," Beowulf is permitted to partake of the cup before Hrothgar's own retainers. This is another honor added to Beowulf.

We remember from Canto IV that Beowulf promised to "purify" Heorot and rid it of the monster. Similarly and materially is Heorot purified after Grendel's vanquishment by the removal of blood-stains and all evidences of the monster. Only the arm is permitted to remain as both trophy and reminder. Thus Heorot is purified in a symbolic way from Sin, as some critics have claimed, and the purification is also carried out physically by the cleaning of the great hall.

CANTO XVI

The giving of gifts is continue in this canto and Hrothgar offers to pay in gold for the man who was killed. Following is a brief reference to the great god, Wyrd, and it is obvious here (once again) that the Anglo-Saxons identified Wyrd and the Christian God into one director of mankind: "The creator ruled the race of men as he still does." Singing is begun and the minor narrative "The Lay of Finn" (also known as the Finn **Episode**) is heard. "Hrothgar's hero," the Scylding Hnaef is killed and the Frisian King, Finn, loses subsequent battle to Hengest. On the funeral pyre of Hnaef, Hildeburh, Danish wife of Finn, places her own sons with great cries of sadness.

Comment

The **episode** concerning Finn, Hengest and Hnaef is the traditional account (see History) of incidents relating to King Hnaef of the Danes and his visit to Finn, King of Frisia. A band of Finn's men treacherously attacked the Danes as they slept in their mead-hall and a fierce fight ensued, lasting five days. This is taken from the **epic**, *The Fight at Finnsburg* (see Chapter on Heroic Literature above) which informs us that during the five days: "... none of the comrades fell and they held the door." We can see that the fight was essentially a stand-off. From *Beowulf* we learn that eventually Hnaef was killed and Hengest (Hnaef's successor) concludes a truce.

It has been suggested that the Finn **Episode** (and *The Fight at Finnsburg*) refer to a historically existent invasion of the Frisians by the Anglo-Saxons in the first half of the fifth century. As we have seen, this tradition is incorporated in Bede's writings, and Bede himself took the tradition from Gildas. Further corroborative evidence (or at least a cross reference) is found in a text of the *Chronicle*.

In *Beowulf* it is suggested that the truce between the Frisians and the Danes is an uneasy one at best: "If any of the Frisians should call this feud to mind by speaking boldly, then the sword-edge shall appease it." We can readily see the two tribes living side by side amidst suspicion and desire for revenge. Finn, according to tradition, is eventually (as we shall see in the next canto) killed by the Danes.

CANTO XVII

The Finn **Episode** continues. Hengest remains all winter with the Frisians while the Danish warriors return home. In the spring the Danish warriors return with reinforcements and Hengest breaks the truce and kills Finn, seizing Hildeburh and Finn's treasure. The scop concludes his song and Wealhtheow appears. A passing reference to Unferth, the thyle (speaker, orator), is made: "He possessed great courage but had not been honorable to his kinsmen in sword-play." Wealhtheow gives the cup to Beowulf who sits between her sons Hrethric and Hrothmund.

Comment

With the conclusion of the Finn **Episode**, Wealhtheow makes another appearance and again gives the cup to Beowulf. She enjoins good fortune upon him and advises him to dispense gifts while he may and leave his fortune and his kingdom to his children. Her advice is somewhat ironical, inasmuch as Beowulf will have no blood descendants, but of course neither Wealhtheow nor Beowulf is aware of the irony.

The parenthetical appearance of Unferth in a place of honor at the foot of his lord is, apparently, in preparation for his later appearance. As we have seen, he is no longer "jealous of glory," but rather "possessed of great courage," or mettlesome spirit, although it is again admitted that he did not use his kinsmen fairly. The contradictory qualities of Unferth sometimes lead the reader to suppose that this enigmatic character is the victim of unfounded rumors because, other than the charges laid against him, he is courageous and generous. Significantly, however, Unferth never denies the charges laid against him which lead the reader to suppose that he possibly has no defense. It is obvious that he is held in a certain awe and fearful respect which could be directly attributable to the terribleness of his crimes.

CANTO XVIII

Wealhtheow gives Beowulf gifts of a corselet, rings, and a magnificent collar which the poet says is: "...the largest of those on earth I have heard tell." The gifts received by Beowulf are compared to the treasure hoard of Hama which included the Brosings's necklace. The collar received by Beowulf will eventually be worn by Beowulf's uncle, Hygelac the Geat, when he falls in a war against the Frisians. Wealhtheow asks Beowulf to be a guide to her sons and again enjoins fortune upon him, long life and happiness. At the end of Wealhtheow's speech, an ominous foreboding of further calamity appears: "... the men drank wine, ignorant of fate or how grim calamity had befallen many men." Hrothgar departs to his court after evening and the warriors sleep in Heorot with their armor as they did in former days according to their custom.

Comment

The speech of Wealhtheow is directly contrasting to the indication of doom appearing in the second half of this canto. Wealhtheow, the "Scylding's dame," is, perhaps, the personification of Woman to an extremely masculine, warlike society. She ever appears as humble, trusting, domestic and subordinate to her lord Hrothgar. Wealhtheow perhaps never becomes so abstract as to be a symbol for Goodness and Virtue but in her pretty speeches, she refers to gentleness, goodness, faithfulness and friendship. If, as St. Augustine contended, woman could be a great spiritual agent for the Good, then Wealhtheow is a clear indication of this in *Beowulf*.

The warriors, unaware that something is about to happen, prepare Heorot by clearing benches and spreading the skins of animals on the floor. Because it is their custom they retire with their arms near them. The warriors, ironically, believe that things have returned to "normal" and everything is the way it "used to be," and so they go to sleep as usual.

CANTO XIX

As we saw before, the price of at least one warrior's rest would be very steep. Grendel's mother, the avenger of her son's death, appears, and her descent is traced from Cain, again referred to as the "first murderer." The warriors are amazed at her appearance: "There was an immediate relapse to the warriors when Grendel's mother rushed in ..." She seizes one of the warriors and retreats to the fen. Significantly, the kidnaped warrior was one of Hrothgar's dearest comrades, a "powerful shield-warrior," and a "prosperous here." Grendel's mother also takes her son's arm down from the wall before she flees. When that is noticed a great cry arises from Heorot.

Beowulf, who has been given his own quarters, is not sleeping at Heorot. He is summoned to the presence of Hrothgar and, ignorant of everything that has been happening, asks Hrothgar in all innocence if he had an easy night.

Comment

The genealogy of Grendel's mother as a descendant of Cain compels a response. Beowulf must do battle in pitulation (as we might expect) of the genealogy of Grendel himself. From the fratricide, Cain, "the first murderer," spring demons, eotins (giants, monsters) and sprites. The underlying motif of evil and accompanying images of darkness and creatures of the underworld appear again.

The aspect of Heorot is changed completely after the appearance of Grendel's mother. Whereas there had been much feasting and merrymaking, now: "... sorrow had become renewed in the dwellings." This has all been prepared by the statements toward the last part of the previous canto (statements that contrast with the optimistic sentiments of Wealhtheow) and demonstrate the impotence and tragic situation of man in the world. That this **theme** need not necessarily be a pessimistic view of the Anglo-Saxons is discussed elsewhere (cf. Introduction to *Beowulf*). Suffice it to say that Beowulf, a believer in wyrd and the Will of God, does not take a pessimistic outlook, indeed, paradoxically opposing faith in himself as hero against the implacable forces around him.

CANTO XX

Hrothgar brushes aside Beowulf's inquiry after his happiness and says that the sorrow of the Danes is renewed. The comrade of Hrothgar, Aeschere, is dead at the hands of Grendel's avenger. Hrothgar recounts an old legend of two monsters that inhibit the moor and walk by night. They are reported to live in a bottomless pool that is not far from Heorot. Hrothgar believes the two monsters of the legend to be Grendel and his mother. Beowulf is asked by Hrothgar to seek out Grendel's mother where she lives and to destroy her. If he performs this second great feat then Hrothgar promises to reward Beowulf even as he did after the defeat of the first monster.

Comment

The female monster, although less powerful that her son, is shielded in her watery retreat, and it is obvious that Beowulf will be at considerable disadvantage should he go there to seek her out. It is not known exactly where Grendel's mother lives, except somewhere in the fathomless pool: "There is living no one so wise of the children of men who knows the bottom."

Thus, while the monster whom Beowulf is to fight is no less territory not his own, with the symbolical interpretation seen by several critics that Grendel's mother (and by implication, Grendel) is identified with Evil, just as Beowulf is identified with Good. Beowulf will fight in the forbidden realms of the powers of darkness and it is suggested that he might not return: "I will reward you with money for your strife and with treasures as I did before and with twisted gold, if you come away." If, as other critics claim, the Beowulf **epic** represents the Christian **theme** of fall and redemption, then Beowulf's descent into the underworld lair of Grendel's mother must surely represent his descent into Hell or, even more symbolically, represent in Germanic form the myth of Christ's descent into Hell. On another level it has been suggested that Beowulf's descent into Grendel's lair is taken from Virgil's account of Aeneas' descent into the nether world. (Evidence for these interpretations depends on a wider textual examination than may be given here but the interested student is advised to refer to the Bibliography for more references on the subject). In any case, the Heroic Tradition determines that Beowulf shall undertake what other men could not and that - because he is different from other men - he has hope of escaping. It is this implication which sustains Beowulf in his role of hero.

CANTO XXI

Beowulf replies (kindly) to Hrothgar's request saying that it is better for all that a friend be avenged rather than mourned. Beowulf philosophically remarks that every man must meet his end and one must do his works before that time, if he hopes for anything in the future. Beowulf promises to seek out the monster and pledges that she shall not escape into the earth's bosom, into the mountain's forests, or under the floor of the ocean. Hrothgar gives him his thanks and accompanies Beowulf with a group of warriors across the moor to the fathomless pool. There they find the bloody head of Aeschere and see firedrakes and sea-dragons swimming in the pool. One of the dragons is killed and brought ashore. Beowulf dons his variegated armor which is "wondrously made ... in days of yore." Unferth generously lends Beowulf his sword, Hrunting, which "never in battle was untrue to any man." Unferth remarks that he had never lent the sword to a better warrior, although it would not be the first time that the sword had achieved a work of valor. Unferth also excuses himself for words spoken when he was in his cups. Since, however, he will not go beneath the waves, his reputation - unlike that of Beowulf - is forfeit.

Comment

The gentle, generous replies of Beowulf before his meeting with Grendel's mother are in sharp contradiction to his boastful statements and promises before he met her son. The character of Unferth has changed, also, from a spiteful provoker to an apologetic and generous comrade. It is almost as if all the characters have been softened by Wealhtheow's admonishment to be gentle. Still, Beowulf does not "care for death," and his belief in wyrd continues to prevail.

Beowulf dons his chain-mail, byrnie (a coat of mail) and hauberk which had been fashioned by a great smith in "days of yore." At once this reference harks back to the Grecian deity Hephaestus, who fashioned the armor of Achilles, and forward to the great armor-smith Trebuchet, who fashioned the armor of so many great knights of the Arthurian cycle.

CANTO XXII

Beowulf announces his readiness and asks Hrothgar to be a guardian of his comrades should he lose his life. He asks also that the treasure he has received be sent back to his lord Hygelac in the event of his death. Beowulf promises Unferth that he will "... obtain fame with Hrunting or be taken by death." Thereupon Beowulf jumps into the pool and descends for nearly a day before he reaches the bottom. He perceives Grendel's mother advancing toward him and she seizes him. Beowulf is protected by his ring-mail but he is clutched so tightly by the monster that he cannot use his weapons. Grendel's mother flees with Beowulf toward her dwelling, and Beowulf sees around him many strange and antagonistic monsters. Finally he finds himself in a "hostile hall," the dwelling place of the monster. Attacking the monster with his sword, Beowulf rings it on her head but its blade is turned aside: Hrunting will do no damage, failing for the first time. Beowulf casts aside the sword and trusts to his strength alone, his hand-grip of power. The she-monster, however, thrusts Beowulf to the ground and tries to stab him with her dagger. Beowulf is protected again by his sturdy ring-mail, without which he should surely have perished.

Comment

The struggle between Beowulf and Grendel's mother assumes a more supernatural aspect here than did the earlier battle. Beowulf plunges into the pool and descends for nearly a day - a superhuman feat in itself - and is protected from harm, when he is in the grasp of the she-monster, by his "wondrously wrought" armor. The armor becomes almost a symbol of a spell of protection enveloping Beowulf, keeping him from harm. Again it is the miraculous armor which protects him from the monster's dagger when otherwise he would have been killed. Beowulf is exhausted, "weary of mood," by his descent into the pool and by his struggles. The she-monster on her home battleground is the stronger of the two combatants and is aided, it seems, by all the full powers of Hell. But just as Beowulf is protected physically from the powers of darkness, so does the decision of "holy God in war triumphant" award to Beowulf victory over Grendel's mother and life. As we shall see, however, it is no mere gift that is given to Beowulf through the decision of God but something held out which must still be won through the efforts of the hero.

CANTO XXIII

On the point of death, Beowulf spies a miraculous sword among the collection of arms. It is a sword fashioned by giants and greater than any weapon ever used by man. Beowulf seizes the sword and severs the monster's head. Beowulf then finds the body of Grendel and cuts its head from its body. Meanwhile, Hrothgar and his warriors, who have remained above, see the pool growing bright with blood and churning. They conclude that Beowulf has died and return sadly to Heorot. Beowulf's companions remain, gazing sadly upon the crimson surface of the water. Beowulf, with the monster's head in one hand, rises, suddenly to the surface where he is joyously received by his comrades. Then all return to Heorot where Beowulf lays down the head at the feet of the king and queen.

Comment

It is interesting that Beowulf severs the head of the dead Grendel, because this incident probably refers to an old pagan belief that the only sure means of killing an ogre was to sever its head from its body with a magic sword. The "magic" sword is one more "miraculous" element in the account of Beowulf's battle with Grendel's mother and stands in contrast to the personal struggle between Beowulf and Grendel, where Beowulf disdained the use of all armor and weapons. In a manner of speaking, the struggle had assumed more abstract proportions, furnishing evidence for those critics who see in Beowulf an allegory of the struggle between Good and Evil. If this interpretation is correct then, as indicated earlier, Beowulf becomes identifiable with Christian Goodness and Grendel's mother becomes the personification (which seems quite likely) of the Dark and Evil and is thwarted in her own region of the Underworld.

Hrothgar and his warriors, from the Christian standpoint, lack faith and, convinced that Beowulf has died, return to Heorot, lamenting. Beowulf's comrades cannot leave, however, so strong is their attachment to their lord but there is little they can do. Perhaps, according to the tradition of comitatus, they realize that they must descend into the depths to avenge Beowulf if he has died, but clearly the task is too great for mortal warriors.

CANTO XXIV

Beowulf offers the head of the monster to Hrothgar and describes the battle that has taken place. He gives Hrothgar the hilt of the miraculous sword taken from Grendel's lair and promises that all are now safe from invasion by the monsters. Hrothgar studies the runic inscriptions on the sword-hilt which is described as the work of giants who existed before the flood. A long sermon on pride is delivered by Hrothgar, and Beowulf, who is eulogized as a benefit to his people and to the Danes, is contrasted to the evil king Heremod who killed his own retainers and perverted the lord-thane institution. Heremod felt no joy and he received no respect from men, regardless of how he advanced in his power. Heremod provides an example of a man who trod upon wrongful paths from whom all will profit by considering his case.

Comment

Inasmuch as the story on the hilt of the miraculous sword is written in runes, it may be taken to pertain to elements of Germanic mythology, although the mythical battle of the giants is a common story in the folklore of many peoples. Interwoven with this is a reference to the flood of the book of Genesis and to the Old-Testament Lord God.

The **theme** of fame is touched upon by Hrothgar as he mentions the fate of the evil king Heremod: "... he departed lonely from the joys of men, the great prince." We remember in the introduction that: "... by deeds of praise shall a man flourish in every tribe." It is only fame that will persist after a man is departed from this earth, and we are reminded of Beowulf's philosophical statement in Canto XXI: "We each must await an end of our life on earth: let him who is able perform great deeds before death; that will be the best for the warrior when he no longer has life." It is, therefore, wise to consider the ultimate fate of a man who disregards the fame of good deeds and surrenders himself to the promptings of pride. Heremod is an example of one governed by pride.

CANTO XXV

The sermon on pride continues, and Hrothgar mentions the arrogance that grows within the breast of him who does evil until he cannot protect himself against the commands of a cursed spirit. A man of this nature forgets the future because he has been given so many glories in the present. Hrothgar advises Beowulf in a paternal manner to avoid these pitfalls, and to choose better, eternal counsels. Hrothgar gives thanks to God for the death of the monsters and invites Beowulf to join the renewed feasting. Eager to return home, Beowulf and his men retire early. Arising early the next morning, Beowulf returns Hrunting to Unferth and gives him his thanks, not mentioning that Hrunting was useless against the monster. This, the poet mentions, is the mark of a great and generous warrior. Finally, Beowulf and his men are ready to depart.

Comment

In Hrothgar's sermon on pride and arrogance, one is reminded of the Biblical passage that admonishes men to do good and beware of the hardening of the heart. Evil, in Hrothgar's sermon, is regarded as a living force which, if not guarded against, may take hold of the spirit. The force of evil is clearly likened to Beowulf's struggle against the Grendels, and Beowulf is warned against falling into the pitfall of thinking that victory over evil is ever completely won by men. Hrothgar says that death will come to Beowulf as it comes to every man, and so it will benefit him to think on these things. This, of course, leads us back to remarks on the meaning of life made earlier by Beowulf.

Beowulf behaves very generously to Unferth and does not upbraid him for lending a weapon that was useless. Beowulf recognizes the good intention of Unferth in giving him the sword and also realizes that no sword of man would have availed in the slaying of the monster.

CANTO XXVI

Beowulf thanks Hrothgar for his hospitality and pledges that he shall always be ready to render assistance to the Danes should it be needed again. Hrothgar replies that he has never in his life heard a more prudent discourse and he praises Beowulf, predicting that one day Beowulf will be a great king. Hrothgar states that Beowulf has brought peace between their peoples. Hrothgar distributes gifts and takes sad leave of Beowulf: "… around the neck he took him, tears fell from him…" Hrothgar's feelings are evidenced in these moving lines: "The man (Beowulf) was so dear to him that he could not restrain the feeling in his breast; but in his heart, held in the bonds of thought, longing after the dear man flamed against blood." Beowulf and his comrades then depart for their boat.

Comment

Hrothgar's leave-taking of Beowulf is one of the most moving passages in all of *Beowulf*. We have seen that Hrothgar regards Beowulf as a son and we are reminded of a poem by William Wordsworth (of the modern era) in which the shepherd Michael takes leave of his own son, Luke: "… we both may live/To see a better day..." This parallels the line in *Beowulf*: "... the grizzly haired prince had hope ... that they might see each other again ... in conference."

In both poems is the indication that both father and son are lost to each other's sight. Hrothgar has a presentiment that he will not see Beowulf again and Michael is hoping he will again see Luke.

CANTO XXVII

The proud warriors go down to the shore where they are familiarly greeted by the coast-guardsman. He does not challenge them but instead remarks that their kinsmen will be very happy to see them when they return. Beowulf presents the coast-guardsman with a sword as a gift and then the warriors embark in their ship, loaded with treasure received from Hrothgar. The treasure is carried to Hygelac, Beowulf's lord. We are informed, in a digression, that the queen of Hygelac is Hygd, daughter of Haereth. Hygd is not a miserly queen and not averse to distributing treasure, unlike the atrocious Thryth, the princess whom nobody but her husband dared look in the face. Offa, of the house of Hemming, put a stop to the executions practiced by Thryth. It is said that she practiced less evil after she was given to this young warrior (Offa) and that eventually she became a wise and just ruler in his court.

Comment

The coast-guardsman appears at the arrival and departure of Beowulf and his companions and is a character whose treatment is less human than Hrothgar, or even than Unferth, and yet who stands out with other briefly appearing characters (such as Wulfgar). He is more real than, for example, King Heremod, or the Frisian Finn. Wulfgar's appearance gives us a bit of insight into the Danish aristocracy and the coast-guardsman permits us insight into the character of the Danish common warrior or yeoman.

Since Beowulf is the thane of Hygelac, it is fitting that the treasure be carried to Hygelac and be distributed by him. Hygelac is described as the "dispenser of treasure," but no further mention of him is made in this canto.

A digression upon the character of Hygelac's queen Hygd is made and a further explanatory digression is made into the character of Thryth, later queen of Offa. Again the modern reader may be taken aback by the seeming lack of unity or the unevenness here, but it must be remembered that these references are pertinent to the audience that either listened to or read Beowulf in much the same way that references contained in the poetry of Robert Browning or T. S. Eliot would be explicable to the educated modern reader.

CANTO XXVIII

Beowulf is greeted by Hygelac and his queen. Hygelac kindly questions Beowulf about what has befallen him and what adventures he has had. Hygelac confesses that he was afraid something might have happened to Beowulf and admits that he prayed Beowulf might not meet the fearful monsters, rather hoping that the Danes would solve their own problems. Hygelac then gives thanks to God for letting him see Beowulf safe and sound again. Beowulf recounts his achievements very briefly and mentions the gifts distributed to the warriors by Wealhtheow. Beowulf also discusses Hrothgar's attempts to secure the peace.

Comment

The fear of Hygelac that Beowulf would not return (or that this was a foolhardy venture) harks back to the intimation in Canto III: "His voyage prudent men somewhat criticized, though he was dear to them." Beowulf recounts his adventures only briefly and the reader is led to suspect that it is to avoid redundancy that another account of the battles is omitted. Beowulf, however, will dwell at length on his deeds in the subsequent chapters and much to the delight of the Anglo-Saxon audience for whom these encounters provided the focal point of their attention. In capacity of political advisor, Beowulf remarks on certain political developments which will be taken up subsequently.

CANTO XXIX

The text - from the end of Canto XXVIII to the beginning of Canto XXX - has been lost entirely.

CANTO XXX

Beowulf is skeptical that peace can be achieved through the efforts of Hrothgar to marry his daughter to Ingeld and the general remarks continue along this line. Beowulf demonstrates how smoldering passions may be fanned into a great flame of war and that the memories of old enmities cannot be buried under even the love of a king for his queen. Beowulf offers his opinion: "Thus, the Heathobards' affection I do not value..." Beowulf suddenly takes up his account of the slaying of Grendel and his mother and faithfully reports all that we have heard earlier.

Comment

Beowulf's remarks on the political conditions are remarkably perspicacious and his point of analysis is largely psychological, that is, his knowledge of men. He characterizes the Heathobards as an impulsive, warlike race who apparently are unaware of what is good for them. Beowulf's remarks contain the implication of the subsequent destruction of the kingdom of Hrothgar. That Beowulf does not care too much for the Heathobards is fairly obvious.

The recapitulation of Beowulf's struggle may be very boring to the modern reader, inasmuch as it contains no really new facts or interpretation. Indeed, it is a simplified version of exactly what we read earlier. Significantly, at the end Beowulf remarks that he triumphed over Grendel's mother because, in his opinion, he was "not yet doomed." This is yet another indication of the Anglo-Saxon concern with Fate and God, which they combined in various admixtures. A positive wyrd is the interpretation given the Will of God acting in his behalf.

CANTO XXXI

Beowulf goes on to describe the gifts he received from Hrothgar. The gifts are brought in and laid before Hygelac, who is one of Beowulf's few near kinsmen. Beowulf presents Hygelac with four matched bay horses and also armor, the poet remarking that this is the way kinsmen ought to behave rather than engaging in dark and subtle plots against one another. It is reported that Beowulf presented Hygd with the necklace given him by queen Wealhtheow and we are informed that Hygd wore it on her breast ever thereafter. We are also informed that Beowulf's reputation had not been great, that he had been looked down upon by his mead-hall companions. Even Hygelac had not really thought him good for much. Beowulf had never killed a drinking companion while he was drunk; he had preserved his great strength until it could be used at the proper time, that is, on the battlefield or against demons and monsters. King Hygelac now presents Beowulf with a sword, the greatest gift that could be given among the Geats. In addition, Beowulf receives seven thousand hides and a mead-hall. In succeeding years, the kingdom of Hygelac and his son, Heardred (who are both killed) devolves upon Beowulf who rules it well for fifty years. When Beowulf is old and approaching the end of his life, a fire-breathing dragon begins to make its presence known.

Comment

The unevenness of Beowulf with respect to time is perfectly obvious in this canto. The death of Hygelac and Heardred and the fifty-year reign of Beowulf are mentioned in a scarce dozen lines as opposed to the several canto interview between Beowulf and Hygelac.

Surprisingly we find that Beowulf was not regarded by the Geats as a great hero and that behind his back - it could not be mentioned publicly since Beowulf was a kinsman of the king - Beowulf was spoken of as a weak and sluggish prince: "For a long time the sons of the Goths did not account him of any good, or (did they consider) the Lord of Hosts would place him on the mead-bench of the worthy ..." That is, that it would turn out badly because Beowulf was not of the stature of the great warriors. This conception of Beowulf parallels the early career of Scyld Sceafing who, as a youth and young man, was regarded as weak and frail, unfit and without origin. It is perhaps of similar importance that Beowulf has few near kinsmen.

Beowulf's nobility of mind and bearing are again cited by the poet when Beowulf gives his relatives gifts. We remember Beowulf's generous treatment of Unferth from whom he had received insults and an impotent sword. The gentleness of Beowulf is clearly identifiable with certain Christian virtues later to become manifest in the "polite knight" of Medieval Romance. Beowulf, "in his cups," (when drunk) never killed a companion and always acted "after judgement" (like the crafty Ulysses) because he was aware of " ... the ample gift of his very great strength that he was given by God." Beowulf now receives the highest honor among the Geats to the great shame of those who had talked behind his back and slandered his reputation.

The canto is ended by an account of the death of Hygelac at the hands of the Swedes which looks forward to certain predictions made at the time of Beowulf's death. A condensed version of Beowulf's fifty-year rule is given and we remember that Hrothgar had ruled for half a century when he was nearing the end of his life. Similarly, Beowulf was "a wise king, an old land-guardian, until a dragon began to hold sway on dark nights." The overtones are in preparation for the account of Beowulf's last struggle.

CANTO XXXII

The thief who stole the cup from the dragon's hoard did not do so out of maliciousness or greed, but rather from necessity. The guilty man was a runaway serf, suffering the displeasure of his master and in need of shelter. He stumbled upon the Dragon's lair by accident and, hoping to appease his master, fled in terror with a jeweled cup. The great treasure hoard of the dragon had remained intact for three centuries. It had been buried there by one of the people's nobles "who there longest wandered, a sad man." The noble hoped for an extension to his earthly days that he might enjoy his treasure a little longer and think back to former times. Finally, the sad old noble died, and a dragon who came to defend the treasure slept undisturbed until the discovery of the stolen cup was made. When the dragon discovered the theft, he ravaged the lands about with fire and destruction. When Beowulf hears of this, he lapses - somewhat incongruously in terms of his previous presentation - into melancholy.

Comment

The fragmentary condition of the manuscript makes portions of this canto somewhat ambiguous and any definite statements concerning the thief are impossible. At least it is known that the theft was performed under "dire necessity," but that is all that may be said non-speculatively. Through some occurrence (here the lines are missing in whole or in part) the Dragon comes to defend the treasure buried by the sad noble.

The section that treats of the noble is called *The Survivor's Lament* and is one of the finest examples of elegiac verse in Old English literature. The passing glories of the earth (his treasure) and his friends and comrades of the sword (whom he will not see again) make the noble sad. His question takes the form of ubi sunt... ?" (That is "where are... ?"). (See the remarks on this **theme** under The Wanderer.) Perhaps, from the standpoint of Hrothgar's sermon, he noble had not thought about the end of life and had not accepted eternal counsels, preferring instead material glories of the earth. The treasure, he does not realize, could make him little other than sad. Or, as some critics believe, a Christian moral of the vanities of the world is interwoven here. In any case the noble is tragically involved in his contemplation of treasure which can bring him neither Christian bliss nor Anglo-Saxon fame (lof, which for a warrior is best to obtain).

When Beowulf hears of the dragon's outrages, he becomes very melancholy: "... his breast boiled within with dark thoughts as was not characteristic of him..." This unexpected reaction on the part of Beowulf is the same reaction undergone by Hrothgar when his kingdom is threatened by Grendel. Beowulf believes that he has in some way offended against God, and he dwells on this subject to the point of brooding. A sharply drawn distinction to the youthful Beowulf!

CANTO XXXIII

When, however, the dragon destroys Beowulf's own home, he vows revenge as if only this deed could awaken him from his melancholic slumbers. We remember that Beowulf said that to avenge was better than to mourn. Preparing to battle the dragon, Beowulf orders an iron shield to be fashioned (rather than a conventional wooden one which would be of no avail against the dragon's fulminations). The previous deeds of Beowulf are mentioned: his struggle against Grendel and his escape from the Battle of Friesland by swimming with thirty sets of armor on his back. It is mentioned also that Beowulf refused the offer of Hygelac's kingdom, preferring to act as an advisor to youthful Heardred until he came of age. When Heardred was killed by rovers who had overcome the king to the Scylfings, Beowulf accepted the throne.

Comment

Beowulf's immediate reaction to the news of the dragon clearly presents the old Beowulf, in contrast to the youthful hero seen earlier. It is only after he personally suffers injury at the hands of the dragon that the heroic spark ignites his will to action. Beowulf vows revenge: "For this (action) the warlike king, the

Weders' prince learned vengeance." The poet labors to show that the older Beowulf is still the same hero as of "days of yore," by recounting feats performed by the hero. Still, Beowulf's prowess has clearly diminished through the passage of time and we are impressed with the notion that this is to be Beowulf's last encounter.

In Beowulf's three struggles, the opposing monsters become less and less personal, less liable to human apprehension. Proceeding from Beowulf's hand-to hand struggle with Grendel, through his Aeneas-like descent into the underworld, and to his present encounter with the fabulous fire-breathing dragon, Beowulf's powers as a man are lessened or translated into aspects of a superhuman, miraculous agency of Good or Hero. It has been suggested by some critics that the dragon represents a civil war that took place among the Geats and if that is the case (and is so understood by the audience) then the melancholy of the generous Beowulf may be understood.

CANTO XXXIV

Mention is made of Beowulf's friendship to Eadgils, a Swedish prince to whose aid he came earlier in his life. It is stated that Beowulf had outlived every conflict and every enmity. With twelve companions and guided by the thief who had stolen the cup, Beowulf goes forth to meet the dragon. The thirteenth man, the thief, goes against his will and with a sad mind because he is aware that he provoked the troubles originally. Only the thief, of course, knows the way to the dragon's lair. Beowulf and his companions sit not far from the cave and Beowulf becomes momentarily saddened because he knows that his end is near: "... his mind was sad, wandering and death dwelling, his doom near at hand which the old man just salute and seek his soul-reward, parting asunder life from body ..." Although Beowulf is aware that his end is near, he does not despair, instead passes through a momentarily lethargic sadness which almost paralyzes his action. Beowulf pauses to say farewell to his friends and his mind turns on melancholy topics.

Beowulf speaks of his youth and the accidental death of Herebald, oldest of the sons of Hrethel, his guardian. Herebald was killed by one of his brother's arrows. This was an inexpiable accident because whatever happened, Herebald must remain unavenged.

Comment

It was the custom in Scandinavia for men of good birth to give their sons into the care of foster-father in order to be educated and thus there is nothing strange or unusual in Beowulf's upbringing by Hrethel. Saddened by the thoughts that his earthly life will soon be over, Beowulf recounts a sad tale from his youth. The accidental murder of Herebald could be punished but the significance resides in the fact that Hrethel cannot avenge the death of his own son since that would mean that he must raise his hand against his own kin. Beowulf's thoughts turn to other situations where no vengeance could be exacted. It was, of course, a principle of Anglo-Saxon law that no vengeance could be exacted for an executed criminal. These elegiac lines in *Beowulf* are reminiscent of *The Survivor's Lament* mentioned earlier.

CANTO XXXV

Beowulf is reminded by Hrethel's heartbreak over Herebald of the struggles between the Swedes and Geats after the death of Hrethel. The sons of Ongentheow, a Swedish king, refused to keep the peace and Beowulf's kinsmen, Haethcyn and Hygelac exacted vengeance for the Swedish outrages. The fighting led to the death of Haethcyn, King of the Geats, and Hygelac - as mentioned earlier - obtained vengeance for his brother's murder when Ongentheow met his end by the hands of Eofer. Beowulf mentions Daeghrefn whom he slew in battle without using his sword but by means of his mighty grip. Beowulf now makes his last beot: "I have undertaken many battles in my youth; I will seek again conflict as a sagacious guardian of my people and gloriously defeat the atrocious spoiler if he will seek me out from his earth-hall."

Beowulf takes a final farewell and then, "bold beneath his helm," advances to meet the dragon. He strikes the dragon with his sword but to no avail. Further, his iron shield does not afford him the hoped - for protection against the dragon's flames.

Comment

The more heroic, less melancholy Beowulf is summoned up by the poet: "He arose then with his shield, the renowned champion bold beneath his helm; he carried his warsark under the rocky heights, trusting in the strength of a single man: this is no enterprise for a coward."

Beowulf's sword does not avail him against the dragon as Hrunting did not avail him against Grendel's mother. The failure of his sword and the lack of protection afforded by his shield indicate that Beowulf's power is limited and deprived of the miraculous: "The shield protected the life of the great prince for less time than he estimated ..." It is noted that his sword bit "less strongly," than was necessary, a further suggestion of the waning powers of Beowulf. Apparently he will not be powerful enough to complete his task. The canto closes with Beowulf encompassed by flames and bereaved of all his thanes - save one who is not afraid to come to his aid.

CANTO XXXVI

A young kinsman of Beowulf, Wiglaf, comes to his aid. Wiglaf is the son of Weohstan, a Swedish prince of the house of Aelfhere. As Wiglaf remembers the character and generosity of Beowulf, he remarks to his companions: "I remember that time when we were drinking mead and we promised our lord in the mead-hall that we would repay him who gave us these rings for our war-equipment if he ever required it of us." To Beowulf, Wiglaf delivers a speech which invigorates the old warrior: "Dear Beowulf, perform as well as you said in your youth that you would, that you would not let your greatness sink while you were alive ..."

Wiglaf, who can restrain himself no longer, impulsively hurls himself into the flames carrying a sword given him by Onela (an heirloom of Eanmund whom his father Weohstan had killed in battle). The dragon, full of anger and wrath, falls upon the two warriors and covers them with flames. The flames consume Wiglaf's wooden shield and he seeks cover under the iron shield of Beowulf. Beowulf's sword, Naegling, fails it user and snaps in the conflict because "it was not granted Geowulf that iron edges might help in battle." For a third and final time the dragon falls upon Beowulf, this time fastening its poisonous fangs into Beowulf's neck.

Comment

Wiglaf, the youthful warrior, is following his lord into battle for the first time. That he is a daring and somewhat reckless youth is evidenced by the fact that he alone, of all the companions who journeyed to the cave, dares to brave the terrible dragon. Wiglaf has reminded his companions of their duty (according to comitatus) but they do not heed. It is seen that the young Wiglaf is possessed of certain qualities we remember in the youthful Beowulf, that is, concern with right-acting and the call of duty.

CANTO XXXVII

Wiglaf displays the "craft and courage" that he had inherited. He does not pay any attention to his hand which is scorched by the dragon's fire. Craftily, he does not strike with his sword at the dragon's head but rather to a more vulnerable place much lower and with such force that the moment his sword penetrates the dragon's hide the terrible fire begins to abate. Beowulf, thereupon regaining command of his senses, takes his dagger and rips open the dragon's belly. Together, lord and thane, they kill the dragon, and, as the poet observes, this is the manner in which men should act. Beowulf is conscious of the effects of venom injected by the bite of the dragon and he sits down to await his end. Wiglaf brings him water and listens to Beowulf as he awaits his impending death: "He knew quite well that he his moments and joy on earth had passed through." Beowulf passes briefly over his career and its vicissitudes in a final speech and asks Wiglaf to show him the treasure hoard that he might die more tranquilly.

Comment

The perfect example of lord-thane relationship, or comitatus, is given and approved here by the poet. Wiglaf risks his own life to save the life and honor of his lord. Fittingly, lord and thane together slay the dragon. Unfortunately, this encounter, as we see, spells the end of Beowulf: it is as the hero expected and in obedience to the all-powerful wyrd. Beowulf says that he can rejoice in his life because he did not swear false oaths, defended what was his and did not pick quarrels: he lived up to the highest Ethic of the Anglo-Saxons. He is happy also that he cannot be accused of the most heinous of all crimes, the murder of his own kin.

Significantly, Beowulf asks to view the treasure. We suspect that the moral of *The Survivor's Lament* may be lost here but this is dispelled when it becomes obvious that the treasure is for Beowulf merely the emblem of his act or the "fruits" of it.

CANTO XXXVIII

Wiglaf quickly obeys the command of Beowulf and goes to the dragon's cave for the treasure. He takes much as of the spoil as he can carry and returns to Beowulf whom he finds on the brink of death. Beowulf looks at the trophies and thanks God that he has been able to acquire such treasure for his people before his death. Beowulf gives direction for the construction of his funeral pyre on Hronesness. He then gives Wiglaf his golden ring, helmet and byrnie and bids him use them well. "You are the last remnant of our race of Waegmundings: destiny has taken all my kinsmen to the Godhead, earls in their valour; I shall follow them." These are the last words of Beowulf.

Comment

Although the warrior-spirit may be observed to have understandably abated in the aged Beowulf, his nobility and generosity have not changed. We remember his remarks to

Hrothgar, that it befits a warrior to do great deeds before the day of his death, and Beowulf - at the moment of his own death - gives thanks that he has performed this last great deed for the benefit of his people before he expired. The ironical implications of his acquisition will become apparent shortly. The noble motives of Beowulf in viewing the treasure are obvious: he wishes it not for himself, or, perhaps, even as an emblem of his fame, but rather for his people. Beowulf appears here as a "shepherd of his flock," as a patriarchal figure.

CANTO XXXIX

Wiglaf laments the death of his hero, lord and kinsman. The dragon which has killed Beowulf lies nearby, lifeless and still bleeding. Legend says that no hero, however courageous, had ever braved the dragon's blasting breath or laid a finger upon its treasure hoard. Once again, the companions of Beowulf appear, coming out of the wood to where they had fled. Wiglaf rebukes the deserters as cowards who had no courage to come to the aid of Beowulf when they might have saved his life. Death is better than the dishonor that will surely follow them, he says.

Comment

The behavior of Beowulf's comrades here (with the exception, of course, of Wiglau) is a contrast to the behavior of the "kindred band" of comrades that rose to Beowulf's defense against Grendel. We remember that Beowulf's comrades in Heorot leap to his defense, although they are of no help. Wiglaf accuses Beowulf's thanes of a breach of comitatus and for this they shall be deprived of all their land and must suffer exile. When other nobles hear of their cowardice, it seems, death will be preferable to their shame of dishonor.

CANTO XL

Wiglaf orders that the results of the struggle be made known to the men who waited on the sea-cliff fort. The messenger tells the men frankly that both Beowulf and the monster have died and that Wiglaf remains a living hero beside the dead. The messenger predicts that the country will be threatened with war when the Franks and Frisians hear of the fall of the hero. According to the messenger, the Franks have been unfavorably disposed since the death of Hygelac, and he does not count on the goodwill of the Swedes either.

Comment

The gloomy predictions of the messenger upon the death of Beowulf hinge upon previously unresolved quarrels. We remember that Wiglaf's sword was taken from a Swedish king by Wiglaf's father and is thus a reminder of an unsettled blood-feud, furnishing the Swedes with an excuse to declare war when Wiglaf assumes the Geat throne. In the sense that Grendel is a harbinger of the disaster which overtakes the Danes, it has been contended that the dragon is a harbinger of a disaster which will subsequently overtake the Geats. This is certainly confirmed by the messenger's statements which are ominous portents.

CANTO XII

The messenger's retrospective account of the struggles between the Swedes, led by Ongentheow, and Hygelac's Geats is continued. Eofor, as mentioned earlier by Beowulf, killed Ongentheow and in so doing won a great reward and also the hand of Hygelac's daughter. The messenger contends that this feud is the basis of the future struggles of the Geats and Swedes.

After listening to the messenger, the entire company rises and goes to view the body of the fallen warrior and also the corpse of the slain dragon. No man dares touch the treasure hoard - except a man of God's own choosing, whomever that might be.

Comment

Although the reason for the enmity of the Swedes has already been suggested, the messenger suggests other possibly more cogent facts which, as we remember, were stated by Beowulf in Canto XXXV.

CANTO XLII

The dragon had wrongfully kept the treasure hoard sealed in the barrow. The princes who placed the treasure in the barrow had pronounced a curse on it that should last until the last day of the world. Wiglaf gives the order that lumber be prepared for Beowulf's funeral pyre. Next he summons seven of the best men and with them enters the dragon's cave. After heaving the dragon over the cliff, the cave is pillaged and the gold loaded onto a wagon.

Comment

The introductory remarks concern the evils of hoarding and then touch upon the uncertainty of life, a **theme** which has pervaded

Beowulf almost from the beginning. The indications of the end of Beowulf - his funeral - become manifest when Wiglaf orders men to bring wood for the funeral pyre.

CANTO XLIII

The Geats prepare a great funeral pyre for Beowulf as he had asked them to do. The pyre is hung about with helmets, shields and byrnies. The mourning soldiers lay Beowulf in the midst and a great funeral fire is lit. The roaring of the flames is mingled with the cries of the mourners until the flames subside and the body of the hero crumbles to pieces. Upon the headland a great mound is built in ten days to be seen by seafarers. In the barrow is placed the cursed treasure, as useless now as it was before. The twelve chieftains, all sons of princes, lament their loss as they ride around the barrow. Beowulf is given a final eulogy: "Thus deplored the Geats the fall of their lord; his hearth-enjoyers said that he was of the family of man mildest, and kindest and to his people the gentlest and of praise most desirous.

Comment

Thus the **epic** of Beowulf returns to a funeral scene which is almost where it had begun. The grandeur of Beowulf's funeral is equal to the funeral of the mythical Scyld Sceafing, mentioned in the first chapter. Ironically, the treasure, which Beowulf wished to win for his people is useless to everyone. This is the final **irony** of *Beowulf*, dealing as it does with the illusion and uncertainty of life against which a hero must strive.

BEOWULF

INDEX OF CHARACTERS

....

Aelfhere: An ancestor of Weohstan and Wiglaf.

Aeschere: Elder brother of Yrmenlaf; Hrothgar's "dear friend," who is killed by Grendel's mother.

Beanstan: Father of Breca.

Beowulf: There are two Beowulfs in the **epic**. One, the first, is the son of Scyld Sceafing and the grandfather of Hrothgar. The other Beowulf, the hero of the poem, is the son of Ecgtheow and nephew of Hygelac (see Genealogy). The first Beowulf is a Dane and the second is a Geat.

Breca: Son of Beanstan and king of the Brondings, with whom, as a young man, Beowulf had his famous swimming contest.

Daeghrefn: Champion of the Franks who was killed by Beowulf with his "grip of iron," when Hygelac invaded the Netherlands and Rhine valley.

Eadgils: A Swedish prince, son of Ohthere and brother of Eanmund. Beowulf came to his assistance when he invaded Sweden.

Eanmund: The brother of Eagdils; killed by Weohstan, father of Wiglaf.

Ecglaf: The father of Unferth.

Ecgtheow: The father of Beowulf the Geat; he married the daughter of Hrethel, father of Hygelac (see Genealogy).

Eofor: The son of Wonred and brother of Wulf; killed the Swedish king Ongentheow.

Eomer: Son of Offa.

Eormenric: Historical king of Ostrogoths.

Finn: King of the Frisians and also ruler of the Jutes; son of Folcwanda and husband of Hildeburh, sister of Hnaef. In a war with Hnaefs Danes, Finn is killed. (See The Fight at Finnsburg.)

Fitela: Son, nephew and companion of Sigemund.

Folcwanda: Father of Finn.

Freawaru: Daughter of Hrothgar; married Ingeld, prince of Heathobards.

Froda: King of the Heathobards and father of Ingeld.

Garmund: Father of Offa.

Grendel: The monster who ravaged Heorot. He descended from Cain.

Guthlaf: A Dane, one of Hnaef's and Hengest's followers.

Haereth: Father of Hygd, wife of Hygelac.

Haethcyn: Son of Hrethel; killed his brother Herebald by accident. Ongentheow, the Swedish king, later killed him.

Halga: Son of Danish king Healfdene.

Hama: A Germanic myth, a hero.

Healfdene: A Danish king, son of Beowulf the Dane, father of Hrothgar.

Heardred: Son of Hygelac and later king of Geats; killed by Swedish king Onela and succeeded by Beowulf the Geat.

Heatholaf: A Wylfing, killed by Ecgtheow.

Hengest: A Danish chief; assumed command of Danes after Hnaef's death.

Heorogar: Son of Healfdene, brother of Hrothgar.

Heoroweard: Son of Danish king Heorogar; nephew of Hrothgar.

Herebald: Geat prince, son of Hrethel; accidentally killed by Haethcyn.

Heremod: A Danish king specifically cited as the negative example of a ruler.

Hildeburh: A Danish princess, daughter of Hoc and wife of Finn; sister of Hnaef, king of Danes.

Hnaef: King of the Danes, killed by Finn's men.

Hoc: The father of Hildeburh.

Hondscio: One of Beowulf's followers, killed by Grendel in Heorot.

Hrethel: A Geat king, father of Hygelac and grandfather of Beowulf.

Hrethric: Son of Hrothgar; later killed by Hrothulf.

Hrothgar: King of Danes; son of Healfdene; brother of Heorogar and Halga; husband of Wealhtheow; father of Hrethric, Hrothmund and Freawaru.

Hrothmund: Son of Hrothgar.

Hrothulf: Nephew of Hrothgar; son of Hrothgar's brother, Halga.

Hunlafing: Danish follower of Hnaef.

Hygd: Wife of Hygelac; daughter of Haereth; mother of Heardred. Her name means "prudence."

Hygelac: Beowulf's uncle and lord; king of Geats; husband of Hygd; father of Heardred.

Ingeld: Prince of unruly Heathobards; son of Froda; married to Freawaru (daughter of Hrothgar). Beowulf does not believe that this political alliance will keep the peace.

Offa: King of the Angles; husband of Thryth.

Ohthere: Son of Ongentheow; brother of Onela; father of Eanmund and Beowulf's friend, Eadgils.

Onela: Swedish king; son of Ongentheow; he killed the Geatish king Heardred; later killed by his nephew (see Genealogies).

Ongentheow: Swedish king; father of Onela and Ohthere; killer of the Geat king Haethdyn; killed by Eofor.

Oslaf: A Danish follower of Hnaef and Hengest.

Scyld Sceafing: The mythological founder of the Danish royal house. Literally his name means "child with sheaf."

Sigemund: Legendary Germanic hero; son of Waels. The story of Sigemund is sung in *Beowulf*.

Wealhtheow: The wife of Hrothgar; called the "peacemaker," and the "Dane's Damsel." The only female figure in *Beowulf* to assume any sort of identity of her own.

Weohstan: Father of Wiglaf; killer of Eanmund, brother of Eagdils who was later to become king of Sweden. The implications of a blood-feud are obvious and mentioned indirectly by the messenger who announces Beowulf's death.

Wiglaf: Son of Weohstan; comes to Beowulf's aid during fight with dragon; subsequent ruler of Geats.

Wonred: Father of Eofor and Wulf.

Wulfgar: A chief of the Wendels and advisor at the court of Hrothgar.

Yrmenlaf: Brother of Aeschere (Hrothgar's friend).

BEOWULF

. . . .

KINGS OF ANGELN AND MERCIA OF THE LINE OF OFFA

```
Woden
  |
Wihtlaeg
  |
Wermund (Garmund)
  |
Offa I. (Uffi) --- Hygd, relic of Hygelac of Hygleik
     | |
  -----------
  |   |
Dan Mykillati, |
King of Denmark | |
        |
        Angeltheow
        |
        Eomer
        |
        Icel
        |
```

Cnebba
|
Cynewald
|
Creoda (593 A.D., England)
|
Wybba
|
Eawa (642 A.D.)
|
Osmod
|
Eanwulf
|
Thingferth
|
Offa II --- Cynethryth (796 A.D.)

THE SCYLDINGS OR DANISH ROYAL HOUSE

Scef
|
Scyld (Sceafing)
|
Beowulf (Beaw, the Dane)
|
Taetwa ^*
|
Geat
|

---

* From Taetwa to Woden, the names are taken from *the Anglo-Saxon Chronicle*, year 855.

```
Godwulf
 |
Finn
 |
Frithuwulf
 |
Frealar
 |
Frithuwald
 |
Woden
 |
 |
Healfdene
------------------------------------------------
 |         |            |             |
Heorogar  Hrothgar --- Wealhtheow   Halga (Helgi)   Ela
 |         | |
 |         | -------------------------------------
 |         |    |     |      |
Heoroweard Ingeld --- Freawaru Hrethric Hrothmund
         (Froda's son)
```

THE GEAT OR GOTHIC ROYAL HOUSE

```
   Hrethel           Swerting
     |                  |
---------------------------------------------------------
  |       |      |             |
Herebeald Haethcyn Hygelac --- Hygd a daughter = Ecgtheow
                      |
        ---------------------------
          |                |
      a daughter --- Eofer  Heardred
```

SCYLFINGS OR SWEDISH ROYAL HOUSE

Ongentheow
   |

   | |
Onela Ohthere --- not named
         |

      | |
   Eanmund   Eadgils

BEOWULF

· ·

There are many views on the complex poems of Anglo-Saxon literature. *Beowulf* is our only native epic, but that is not our reason for studying it. For centuries it was forgotten, and even when it was published and studied in the nineteenth century it was considered the product of a barbarous age at best. Critical opinion has raised the reputation of *Beowulf* and other Old English poems a great deal in our time. Anglo-Saxons of the time of the *Beowulf*-poet were a sophisticated people who had developed a complex literature which includes a number of poems ranking with the greatest works in the language. Below we shall consider some of the most important critical statements on Beowulf.

ANTHOLOGY OF CRITICAL VIEWS

Some of the best critical articles on *Beowulf* have been collected in *An Anthology of Beowulf Criticism*, edited by Lewis E. Nicholson (University of Notre Dame Press, 1963, paperback). It includes eighteen scholarly and critical essays on *Beowulf*, representing the earliest and latest critical views.

Briefly, these are the views:

1. F. A. Blackburn, "The Christian Coloring of Beowulf." This essay appeared in 1897 and presented the view - typical among critics of the time - of the poem as being of no poetic value. The Christian element was seen as the "coloring" by a later editor, something acquired later than the original creation. The essay concerned itself (like the one by Chadwick which follows) more with the origins of the poem than with the text itself. Blackburn and Chadwick see the *Beowulf*-poet as a heathen whose work fell later into the hands of a Christian minstrel or scribe who wished to make it Christian. This led to what are held to be inconsistencies in the text.

2. H. Munro Chadwick. *The Homeric Age*, an excerpt. Chadwick (mentioned above), on the basis of studies of around seventy Christian passages in *Beowulf*, argues that the heathen poet knew very little about Christianity.

3. Levin L. Schucking, "The Ideal of Kingship in *Beowulf*." Schucking, like Hamilton (below), holds a view contrary to those mentioned of Blackburn and Chadwick. The *Beowulf*-poet is seen as a Christian reshaper of heathen Germanic traditions of the warrior-ethic which runs through the poem. The ideal of kingship is defined largely in terms of the writings of the church: the "rex justus" (just king) of Augustine.

4. Marie Padgett Hamilton, "The Religious Principle in *Beowulf*." (Mentioned above). Hamilton argues that the

poet reinterprets his own Germanic background in light of the Christian (Augustinian) view of history.

5. J. R. R. Tolkien, *Beowulf*, "The Monsters and the Critics." Tolkien's essay represents the beginning of the new criticism of *Beowulf*, for it challenges the previously held view that the poem had little organic unity - little structure - and was held together only through the character of the central hero. The monsters in the poem represent evil and chaos and are therefore the center of the action, but the real subject is the tragedy of the human condition. He sees a symbolic unity in the poem, a rise and fall, "a balance of ends and beginnings" and "the moving contrast of youth and age."

6. H. L. Rogers, "Beowulf's Three Great Fights." Rogers does not disagree with Tolkien about the **theme** of the poem, but he believes that the poem is not an artistic unity due to the poet's inability to impose his moral ideas on his source. The poem is not, as Tolkien suggests, an "opposition of ends and beginnings" but a progression in Beowulf's three major fights. Rogers examines the motifs of weapons, treasure and society in the poem, and he sees the second and third fights as less successful artistically than the first.

7. Margaret E. Goldsmith, "The Christian Perspective in *Beowulf*." Goldsmith is not in agreement with Rogers' attack on the failure of the poet to impose his moral ideas on his source, saying: "if a martial **epic** of Beowulf was known to our poet, he has taken pains to recast it in quite another mold." She sees the war-descriptions, banquets and swimming feats as the poet's way of expressing the eternal aspects of existence, the moral aspects largely.

8. Kemp Malone, "*Beowulf*." He sees a unity in the two parts of the poem through the poet's patriotism for "Germania" and the spiritual quality of *Beowulf*. The poet himself is a patriotic Englishman. Malone analyzes the poem in terms of its episodes, rather than its general plot.

9. R. E. Kaske, "Sapienta et Fortitudo as the Controlling **Theme** of *Beowulf*." An examination of the **themes** of wisdom and strength, showing the fusion of Germanic and Christian concepts. The article argues that the poem is thematically unified.

10. Herbert G. Wright, "Good and Evil; Light and Darkness; Joy and Sorrow in *Beowulf*." Wright defends the unity of *Beowulf* on purely textual grounds (unlike many critics, such as most of those mentioned above, who argue from evidence of social and literary history and from Biblical exegesis). He sees the poem's unity as being accomplished through an interrelation of **imagery** of opposites: light and darkness, which are concrete effects related to good and evil, joy and sorrow. (This essay calls into question the view of some critics who hold that the analysis of the poem as a unity is oversubtle; such a view is presented by T. M. Gang, "Approaches to *Beowulf*," Review of English Studies, New Series III (1952), pp. 1–12.)

11. Morton Bloomfield, "*Beowulf* and Christian Allegory: An Interpretation of Unferth." Bloomfield argues that the character of Unferth (which has received more and more attention as a significant figure in the poem) is intended to have allegorical significance as a personification of the abstraction of Discordia. This conclusion is drawn on the basis of a comparison with the allegorical method

in Christian Latin poetry. Bloomfield points out that this interpretation is in keeping with the statements of Schucking (mentioned above) on the ideal of kingship based on the Augustinian conception of the perfect ruler. For other articles on the importance of Unferth in Beowulf, see: James L. Rosier, "Design for Treachery: The Unferth Intrigue," Publications of the *Modern Language Association of America* (*PMLA*), LXXVI (March 1962), pp. 1–7. Rosier sees the Unferth design for treachery as of equal importance with the Grendel **episode**. "Grendel and his mother pose an external threat to the stability of the hall (Heorot), whereas Hrothulf and Unferth represent an internal menace." He sees several points of likeness between Unferth and Grendel. Rosier agrees basically with the Bloomfield interpretation cited above, though he sees the Christian - allegorical view as "unnecessary, if not unjust to the more literal but dramatic design of the poet." For an answer to the Rosier interpretation, see: J. D. A. Ogilvy, "Unferth: Foil to *Beowulf*?", *PMLA*, LXXIX (September 1964), pp. 350–375. Ogilvy suggests possibilities other than those in Rosier, implying that Unferth is not so evil as we may assume. (Much of the debate rests on the reading of the title given to Unferth: thyle, which usually is defined as "spokesman or orator, but is redefined by Rosier as being a pejorative title).

Unferth is acquitted of much of his wickedness by another critic: Norman E. Eliason, "The thyle and Scop in *Beowulf*," *Speculum*, XXXVIII (1963), pp. 267–284. Note that Bloomfield has another article in this book, "Patristics and Old English Literature," which demonstrates the significance of the Latin fathers in Old English literature.

12. C. L. Wrenn, "Sutton Hoo and *Beowulf*." Prof. Wrenn systematically examines the evidence of the archeological discovery of Sutton Hoo (the standard, the shield, the helmet, and the musical instrument), showing that the findings were ritually significant, and that they are helpful in our study of *Beowulf*. For further information on Sutton Hoo, see Roger H. Hodgkin, *A History of the Anglo-Saxons* (3rd ed., London: Oxford University Press, 1953), II, pp. 696–734: the authoritative survey of the Sutton Hoo ship in Bruce-Mitford's Appendix. Also, on the importance of the harp in reading Old English poetry, see J. B. Bessinger, "*Beowulf* and the Harp at Sutton Hoo," *University of Toronto Quarterly* (January 1958).

13. Francis P. Magoun, Jr., "The Oral Formulaic Character of Anglo-Saxon Poetry." This is an important and controversial study which has led to a new school of Anglo-Saxon literary criticism. Magoun analyzes lines 1–25 of *Beowulf* and lines 512–535 of Christ and Satan to show the oral formulaic patterns in the poetry.

14. Paull F. Baum, "The *Beowulf* Poet." Baum examines the role of the poet behind *Beowulf*, focusing on the demands on an audience which the poem must have made. The poet "adopted a tense crowded style and a convoluted method of narration, the very antithesis of a minstrel's, most unsuited for recitation, and if he looked for an audience of listeners he was extraordinarily, not to say stubbornly, sanguine." The portrait is one of a highly individualistic poet - not the stereotype one usually imagines as the person of a minstrel or scop.

The other articles in the collection include: D. W. Robertson, Jr., "The Doctrine of Charity in Medieval Literary Gardens: A Topical Approach Through Symbolism and Allegory"; Allen Cabaniss, "*Beowulf* and the Liturgy"; M. B. McNamee, S.J., "*Beowulf* - An Allegory of Salvation?"

BEOWULF

. . . .

Question: In your opinion, are the historical digressions (for example, *The Fight at Finnsburg*) in *Beowulf* conducive to the "unity" of the **epic** or not?

Answer: In terms of modern criticism, the digressions of *Beowulf* are sometimes not considered conducive to the unity of the poem because they are occasionally repetitious (as the account of Eofer's struggle with Ongentheow) or they seem to pertain little to the matter at hand (for example, the account given of Thryth, wife of Offa, when Hygd is the subject under discussion). Modern scholars, however, have demonstrated that many of the digressions were exceedingly a propos to the Anglo-Saxon audience to which they were addressed. These digressions served to unify *Beowulf* with a common body of tradition and with facts that were certainly well known to an educated audience. This may be likened to our appreciation of Leo Tolstoy's *War and Peace* from our familiarization with the facts of the Napoleonic Wars. Also, these digressions formed part of the poet's technique. By mention of certain historical facts, the poet is able at times to introduce **irony** into his work. An example would be in the description of Hrothgar's wondrous hall, Heorot, which "unfriendly fire awaits." This clearly refers to a future time when Hrothgar's kingdom is invaded. In addition, some critics have shown that the heroic elements of these fragments offer meaningful parables with the life and character of Beowulf.

Question: How would you resolve the apparent contradiction between the elements of Christian faith and Teutonic myth that appear in *Beowulf*?

Answer: Historically the intermingling of Christian and Teutonic elements in *Beowulf* occurs because this intermingling of beliefs was also true of Anglo-Saxon society at this time. The conversion of the Anglo-Saxons did not take place until little more than a century before the composition of *Beowulf* and it is easy to see that the Germanic traditions could not be - and were not according to the policy of the Roman Church - stamped out immediately.

Question: Why does Wiglaf decree that the men who deserted Beowulf when he went to meet the Dragon shall suffer loss of their lands and exile? Explain in terms of Anglo-Saxon custom.

Answer: The men who deserted their lord on the battlefield were guilty of violating the lord-thane relationship. This relationship, an old Germanic custom - called comitatus by Tacitus - provided that young men attach themselves to some mature warrior. Their obligation was to provide the lord with their services on the battlefield. The obligation of the lord was to provide protection for each man and a share of all bounty or treasure. It was considered an extreme dishonor for a thane to leave the battlefield before his lord, and an extreme dishonor for the lord if he did not excel all his thanes in valor. This institution, which is similar to the later feudal institution, was of extreme importance to the Anglo-Saxons. Wiglaf, we remember, remarks that "death is better than such dishonor," that is, violation of comitatus.

Question: Explain the meaning and function of kenning.

Answer: The kenning is a poetical device whereby a figurative phrase is substituted for a direct reference to the object itself, such as "battle-flasher" for "sword," and "whale road" for "sea." Kenning tends to be an exaggeration of the poetic tendency to synthesize experience but does not necessarily restrict itself to less sophisticated poetry. Examples of kenning (in the form of euphuism) persist in the lyrics of the eighteenth-century English Augustans, such as Pope's use of "finny breed" for "fish." The peculiar circumstance that rendered kenning so common in *Beowulf* is the four-beat alliterative line which was very strictly adhered to as part of the scop's tradition. Such restrictions on the flow of language naturally resulted in the substitution of two-beat phrases in the form of kennings for ordinary words that would not fit into the line.

Question: Relate *Beowulf* to the conventional idea of the "epic."

Answer: There is no single quality which defines an **epic**, and all epics have their distinctive qualities. Usually **epics** are divided into primary and secondary. *Beowulf* is a primary **epic** in that it is not (as far as we know) modeled after classical examples like the Iliad. It arose out of an oral tradition, like the Iliad, and it is not literary in origin. *Beowulf* is considered an **epic** on the grounds that it was written in an exalted, dignified style; has a complex **theme** and narrative which recapitulate the significant preoccupations and experiences of the heroic epoch in Anglo-Saxon tradition; presents a hero who is the epitome of a nation and culture; and links the heroic deeds of the hero with the whole history and tradition of a people. *Beowulf* is the focal point of the whole work, as Achilles is the focal point of the *Iliad*. The poet concentrates on a specific section of the hero's life (or on two sections, unified in **theme** and quality). And we see *Beowulf* in relation to the history of the important peoples: Scyld Sceafing and the Scyldings, the struggle between the Danes and the Heathobards, etc. And the style (the **epic** "high style") of the work is elaborate and rhetorical in a way which embodies the spirit of its heroic subject.

Question: Who was the scop and what was his role?

Answer: Early written literatures are almost always the product of a long oral tradition which developed out of songs and spoken poems. In the case of Anglo-Saxon literature, the oral tradition goes back to the Germanic tribes which inhabited the Continent. The scop (literally "sharper") was a poet-singer who wandered to various courts in search of a patron among the lords. The role of the poet was to entertain during feasts, singing lyrical or heroical poems. He sang of real and legendary heroes whose names lived on because of the song. In *Beowulf* a scop sings at Hrothgar's court about Sigemund (the Volsung) and his heroic defeat of the dragon. But the subject matter of the scop - at least the subject matter which has survived in the manuscripts (dating from around A.D. 1000) - became influenced by Christian notions and adapted traditions of the heroic age according to Christian interpretations.

Question: Is it likely that the *Beowulf* poet looked to contemporary events for his inspiration and subject matter? If so, would you consider his poem a sort of social criticism in the sense, say, of Shaw's or Brecht's plays?

Answer: Most scholars agree that the *Beowulf* legend comes out of a period long before the date of the poem's composition. The poem makes use of a heroic tradition which came down to the poet and his audience through a long oral tradition. Of course it is possible that the legend is based upon real historical events, but whatever actuality stands behind the poem has clearly been embellished in a way clearly separated from historical events. The story of *Beowulf* is mythical in much the sense that the *Tale of Troy* is mythical in its uses by Homer and, for that matter, the 14th century Chaucer in Troilus and Criseyda. The *Beowulf* poet was concerned with finding a significant story - one that would embody and render meaningful the elements of his audience and himself in a way that made poetry or "song." As Lord Raglan argues in his book, *The Hero*, a people, especially at the time of *Beowulf*, can completely forget their actual past within a century and a half. This fact seems to partially explain the tendency of poets to turn to myth, for it remains long after historical facts have faded. As Professor Gilbert Murray argues in *The Rise of the Greek **Epic***, *Beowulf* is like the Homeric poems in that neither refers to specific warfare or other "heroic" events in their recent history. He concluded that this seems "to be the natural tendency of a poet, at least of an **epic** poet." But there remains the question of the function of the poem in terms of the society: does it amount to "social criticism"? There has been little general agreement among readers on this point. For on one hand there seems to be an establishment of heroic values which could almost serve as doctrine to the audience of the poet, as we have seen in "The Wanderer": "A councilor must be patient,/ not too impetuous nor too hasty of speech/ not too weak in war nor too reckless/ nor too timid nor too venturesome nor too greedy/ nor ever too ready to make boasts before he understands them." And on the other hand *Beowulf* was a sort of song (or perhaps symphony is closer to the fact) which the wandering poet or scop sang (probably to a harp like the one found in Sutton Hoo) in order to entertain his audience. It is highly unlikely that the poet saw himself as a social reformer in the sense of a Shaw, for, whereas Shaw is dramatized ideas designed to bring society some sort of salvation, *Beowulf* is an epic recapitulation of the significant ideals and progress of a people, and it is a poem.

Question: What contribution has *Beowulf* made to our understanding of the early civilization in England?

Is it possible to draw specific conclusions about the customs and ways of life from the poem alone?

Answer: Out knowledge of Anglo-Saxon civilization has been an interpretation based on historical records and the literature of the time. For many years historians and anthropologists and literary scholars (the only readers of *Beowulf* until quite recently) conjectured and arrived at strikingly different views of Old English life. Was the famous burial scene in *Beowulf* a true description of the elaborate rites of the time (or an earlier time) or was it a fantastic invention by the poet to embellish a historical past and thereby glorify the nation? It is probably true, as some critics have argued, that *Beowulf* is a patriotic poem, designed to exalt the virtues and achievements of the people. But this does not prevent some of the detail - and a great deal of it - from being accurate transcription of life of the past (the poet's past, rather than his contemporary civilization). Archeological discoveries, especially Sutton Hoo, have led us to believe that detailed descriptions such as that of the burial in the poem are not fantastic after all. The burial ship found at Sutton Hoo contained extraordinary riches, and the articles, as Prof. Wrenn and others have shown, contribute to our understanding of the poem and its relation to the civilization. Before *Beowulf* the only extensive written record we have of the Germanic peoples is Tacitus' *Germania*, completed in A.D. 97–98. *Beowulf* confirms a good deal of what Tacitus said. An example of this is what Tacitus called the comitatus - the relationship of the warrior to his lord, instances of which abound in the poem. We recall that, at the end of *Beowulf*, when the hero is deserted by his men - except for the noble Wiglaf - and left to die in battle, Wiglaf curses the people and tells them that their wealth and land is thereby taken from them. For they have violated a sacred relationship. Wiglaf notes that a warrior's death is highly preferable to the dishonorable one they will endure. In a sense, therefore, *Beowulf* represents a dramatic version of many of the ideals and aspirations of the people. We note that the dramatis personae of the poem are warriors and their enemies - not the common people of the time. In this respect the poem only gives us a partial picture of the civilization: the noble, the controlling element of the society. But we are given an understanding of feudalism - with its highly stratified social relationships and its implications for the whole society. We are also given a background for understanding, for the first time, the confrontation of Roman law and classical civilization with feudalism - a way of life which could not lend itself to the Roman ideals, such as the divine right of kings. Also, *Beowulf* gives us many details of the customs which do not immediately seem relevant, such as (in the words of Professor Chadwick in *The Heroic Age*, Cambridge, 1912, p. 82) "the long detailed account of Beowulf's arrival at the Danish king's hall, and the conversation which the chamberlain holds with the king on the one hand and the visitor on the other, before the latter is invited to enter." This custom of keeping someone standing at the door is related by Lord Raglan, in *The Hero*, to ritual drama (which he holds to be the source of myths, as opposed to historical events as the source of myths). In ritual drama the setting is very often a doorway (or a gateway). Lord Raglan concludes (*The Hero*, Vintage Books, 1956, p. 255): "The reason for this is probably that the ritual was originally performed at the king's palace or tomb, which was often the same place."

This example from Beowulf and from conclusions drawn from it demonstrates another way in which the poem aids our understanding of early civilization and the myths and literature they produced. Thus we do learn a great deal about the people from the poem, but our knowledge only becomes complete - if it ever does - as we combine our findings with the discoveries of history and of literatures in general.

BIBLIOGRAPHY

BOOK LENGTH STUDIES OF BEOWULF

Among the more important books on Beowulf are the following:

1. Arthur G. Brodeur, *The Art of* Beowulf, Berkeley, California 1959. This is an important study which, except for the chapter on **Diction**, can be read without a knowledge of Old English. Among the points of study are: Variation, Structure and Unity, Christian and Pagan, **Episodes** and Digressions, etc.

2. Raymond W. Chambers, Beowulf: *An Introduction to the Study of the Poem with a Discussion of the Stories of Offa and Finn*; 3rd ed., revised by Charles L. Wrenn, Cambridge, 1959. An important work for advanced students; it has an extensive bibliography.

3. William W. Lawrence, Beowulf *and* **Epic** *Tradition*; Cambridge, Massachusetts, 1928. This is a highly scholarly study of the **epic** elements brought together in the poem.

4. John A. Nist, *The Structure and Texture of* Beowulf; Sao Paulo, Brazil, 1959. A readable evaluation with simple synopsis of the poem, discussing structure, texture and metrics.

ARTICLES ON BEOWULF

The student of *Beowulf* should consult the *PMLA* and other cumulative indexes in the library for articles on *Beowulf*. Here is a partial list of important statements on the structure and unity of the poem:

1. Arthur E. Du Bois, "The Unity of *Beowulf*," *PMLA*, XLIX (1934), 374–405.

2. Joan Bloomfield, "The Style and Structure of *Beowulf*," *Review of English Studies*, XIV (1938), 396–403.

3. Adrien Bonjour, *The Digressions in Beowulf*, Medium Aevum Monographs, V, Oxford, 1950.

4. J. L. N. O'Loughlin, "*Beowulf* - Its Unity and Purpose," *Medium Aevum*, XXI (1952), 1–13.

5. Arthur G. Brodeur, "The Structure and Unity of *Beowulf*," *PMLA*, LXVIII (1953), 1183–95.

6. Peter F. Fisher, "The Trials of the **Epic** Hero in *Beowulf*," *PMLA*, LXXIII (1958), 171–83.

ON SPECIFIC ASPECTS OF BEOWULF

1. Arthur E. Du Bois, "The Dragon in *Beowulf*," *PMLA*, LXXII (1957), 819–22. Arguing that the Dragon is an image of civil war, he states that an image acquires meaning in five ways.

2. Tom B. Haber, *A Comparative Study of* Beowulf *and the* Aeneid, Princeton, New Jersey, 1931. Argues that the Beowulf-poet is indebted to Virgil.

3. Robert M. Lumiansky, "The Dramatic Audience in *Beowulf*," *Journal of English and Germanic Philology*, LI (1952), 545–550.

4. Kenneth Sisam, "Beowulf's Fight with the Dragon," *Review of English Studies*, New Series IX (1958), 129–40.

5. Dorothy Whitelock, *The Audience of* Beowulf, Oxford, 1951.

TRANSLATIONS

There are a number of adequate translations, each one attempting to reconstruct the effect of the poem in a different way. The student should compare at least two translations:

1. David Wright, *Beowulf* (Penguin Classics L. 70, New York, 1957). Very readable, in modern prose, with interesting introduction and discussion of the problems of translation.

2. J. R. Clark Hall and C. L. Wrenn, *Beowulf* and the Finnesburg Fragment (London, 1950). An excellent translation, attempting to recapture some of the character of the original.

3. R. K. Gordon, Anglo-Saxon Poetry (Everyman's Library 794, New York, 1962). Has reliable translations of *Beowulf* and other Old English poetry.

4. Edwin Morgan, *Beowulf* (Berkeley, 1962).

BILINGUAL EDITION

A good paperback bilingual edition, with the Old and Modern English juxtaposed by the half-line, which will enable the beginning student of

Anglo-Saxon to enter rather painlessly into the original text: Beowulf *together with* Widsith *and* the Fight at Finnesburg, *The Benjamin Thorper Transcription and Word-for-Word Translation*, with Introduction by Vincent F. Hopper (Baron's Educational Series, Great Neck, N.Y., 1962).

IMPORTANT MODERN EDITIONS IN ANGLO-SAXON

1. Fr. Klaeber, Beowulf *and* the Fight at Finnesburg, 3rd ed., Boston, 1936. Supplements 1941, 1950. The preferred edition with extensive notes, introduction, glossary, and annotated bibliography.

2. Charles L. Wrenn, Beowulf: *With* the Finnesburg Fragment, London, 1953; revised and enlarged, 1958. Extremely important edition with highly useful introduction.

OLD ENGLISH GRAMMARS

The student wishing to learn Anglo-Saxon should use one of the following grammars. In addition, he will find it extremely useful to listen to the recordings listed below of Old English poetry.

1. Randolph Quirk and C. L. Wrenn, *An Old English Grammar*, 2nd ed., London, 1958. Clear, easy to use grammar with special emphasis on the importance of syntax.

2. Alistair Campbell, *Old English Grammar*, London, 1959. More for the specialist.

DICTIONARY

The most readily available is: J. R. Clark Hall, *A Concise Anglo-Saxon Dictionary*, Cambridge, 1931.

BACKGROUND MATERIAL

Among the many useful books, there are the following:

1. David Zesmer, *Guide to English Literature From* Beowulf *through Chaucer and Medieval Drama*, (College Outline Series No. 53, Barnes and Noble, New York, 1961). An extremely useful introduction with extensive annotated bibliographies.

2. Peter H. Blair, *An Introduction to Anglo-Saxon England*, (Cambridge, England, 1960). A good introduction for the general reader to political, social, economic and ecclesiastical history of the period.

SPECIAL ARTICLES

Among the articles referred to in this book are the following two:

1. C. L. Wrenn, "On the Continuity of English Poetry," *Anglia*, LXXVI (1958), 49–59. Prof. Wrenn argues that there has been a greater continuity in the tradition of English poetry than is usually presumed, especially in metrical patterns and in subject matter, thought and mood.

2. James L. Rosier, "The Literal-Figurative Identity of The Wanderer," *PMLA*, LXXIX (September 1964), pp. 366–370. A brilliant analysis of *The Wanderer* using the principles of generative composition: see explanation in The Elements of Anglo-Saxon Poetry in this guide.

RECORDING

There are a number of recordings of readings of Old English, the best of which is J. B. Bessinger's on Caedmon Records. Prof. Bessinger's readings are alive in a way which gets across the qualities of poetry in Caedmon's Hymn (sung with a Sutton Hoo type of harp), *The Wanderer*, parts of *Beowulf*, A *Dream of the Rood*, and *The Battle of Brunanburh*. The readings demonstrate the complex music which is undoubtedly present - in different ways - in each of the poems. Highly recommended.

Printed by BoD™in Norderstedt, Germany